All Wrapped Up™
Coordinated Gift-Wrap Sets in a Snap

Edited by Vicki Blizzard

All Wrapped Up™
Coordinated Gift-Wrap Sets in a Snap

In my opinion, the presentation of a gift is almost as important as the gift itself. I love taking the extra time to make sure all of my gifts are lovingly wrapped and tied prettily in a bow with a matching gift card attached.

If you're like me, you'll love the projects in this book!

Here are 85 ways to give gifts—tucked into bags, covered with interesting wraps or placed in a keepsake box that becomes part of the gift!

While some of these projects do take a little bit of time, they're all easy to create and will add so much to the gifts you give to family and friends.

As you look through this book, you're sure to find just the right wrapping for those special gift-giving occasions!

Warm reguards,

Vicki Blizzard

CONTENTS

3 Bags

38 Wraps

57 Boxes

92 General Instructions

94 Buyers Guide

95 Designer Listing

STAFF
Editor: Vicki Blizzard
Associate Editor: Lisa M. Fosnaugh
Copy Editors: Michelle Beck, Conor Allen
Technical Editor: Brooke Smith
Graphic Arts Supervisor: Ronda Bechinski
Graphic Artist: Vicki Staggs
Assistant Art Director: Karen Allen
Photography: Carl Clark, Matt Owen, Nancy Sharp
Photo Stylist: Tammy Nussbaum

Annie's Attic®
306 East Parr Road, Berne, IN 46711
© 2005 Annie's Attic

TOLL-FREE ORDER LINE or to request a free catalog (800) LV-ANNIE (800) 582-6643
Customer Service (800) AT-ANNIE (800) 282-6643, Fax (800) 882-6643,
Pattern Services (260) 589-4000, ext. 333

Visit www.AnniesAttic.com

All Wrapped Up—Coordinating Gift Sets in a Snap, is published by Annie's Attic, 306 East Parr Road, Berne, IN 46711, telephone (260) 589-4000. Printed in USA. Copyright © 2005 Annie's Attic.

RETAILERS: If you would like to carry this pattern book or any other Annie's Attic publications, call the Wholesale Department at Annie's Attic to set up a direct account: (903) 636-4303. Also, request a complete listing of publications available from Annie's Attic.

Every effort has been made to ensure that the instructions in this pattern book are complete and accurate. We cannot, however, take responsibility for human error, typographical mistakes or variations in individual work.

All rights reserved. Printed in USA
ISBN: 1-59635-020-2
Library of Congress: 2004116368
1 2 3 4 5 6 7 8 9

Spring Butterfly Bag

Design by SUSAN STRINGFELLOW

Pretty pastels and a lovely stamped butterfly make this the right bag for a "just because" gift.

Cut a 4 x 4¼-inch piece of purple card stock; cut a ½ x 4-inch strip of striped paper. Cut a ¼ x 4-inch strip of striped paper. Attach both striped pieces to bottom of purple card stock. Cut a 2 x 2½-inch piece of striped paper and adhere above striped pieces. Layer purple rectangle onto light blue card stock; trim edges.

Stamp the butterfly image toward the upper right corner of rectangle. Stamp sentiment rubber stamp onto light blue card stock; punch out a 1-inch square around words and mount onto white card stock. Trim edges and adhere in lower right corner of purple rectangle.

Cut three 5-inch lengths of fibers; attach them to the left side of card stock and adhere assembled piece to gift bag.

SOURCES: Striped paper from Making Memories; rubber stamps from Stampin' Up!.

MATERIALS
Small purple gift bag
Light blue, purple and white card stock
Coordinating striped paper
Butterfly and sentiment rubber stamps
Black ink pad
Purple fibers
1-inch square punch
Glue stick

⊢ BAGS ⊣

Wedding Gift Trio

Designs by SANDY ROLLINGER

MATERIALS
- 5 x 7-inch white card with envelope
- 8 x 10-inch white gift bag
- White and pink card stock
- Pink vellum
- Opalescent pink paper
- White pearl with ribbon trim
- White pearl trim
- Light pink and opalescent white paper paints
- 8 white heart-shaped buttons
- 2½-inch heart cookie cutter
- ¼-inch-wide pink satin ribbon
- ⅛-inch hole punch
- Heart punch
- Wire cutters
- Double-sided adhesive sheets
- Adhesive foam squares
- Gem adhesive
- Paper trimmer
- Nonstick scissors
- Decorative-edge scissors

Treat your favorite bride and groom to a lovely gift packaged in a set you created just for them!

Gift Bag

Use nonstick scissors to cut a 6 x 6½-inch rectangle from double-sided adhesive sheet. Attach sheet to the back of a piece of opalescent pink paper. Trim edges even and attach to center of the bag. Use gem adhesive to adhere the pearl with ribbon trim around rectangle's perimeter; remove shanks from heart buttons with wire cutters and adhere one heart button to each corner of trim.

Cut a 4 x 5-inch rectangle from vellum with decorative-edge scissors. Punch out holes along edges to give a lacy effect. Apply a small piece of adhesive sheet to the center of vellum and attach to center of bag. Add dots to vellum rectangle with pink paper paint.

Use heart cookie cutter to trace a heart onto pink card stock; trace same heart onto adhesive sheet and cut out with nonstick scissors. Attach pink heart to adhesive heart. Trace and cut one additional heart from opalescent paper; attach opalescent heart to the other side of adhesive sheet heart. Attach pearl with ribbon trim around the perimeter with gem adhesive; let dry and attach heart to center of bag with adhesive foam squares. Glue a heart button to center of heart and embellish with white paper paint.

For gift tag, cut a 2 x 6-inch rectangle from opalescent pink paper; score and fold in half. Use decorative-edge scissors to cut a piece of vellum slightly smaller than tag front. Punch holes along vellum edges and punch out three hearts in center of vellum. Glue punched vellum onto gift tag; add dots to vellum with pink paper paint; let dry. Punch a hole in upper left corner of tag; thread satin ribbon through hole and tie to bag handle.

Card

Follow instructions for gift bag but use a 4 x 5-inch opalescent pink rectangle and a 3½ x 4-inch vellum rectangle. Glue pearl trim around perimeter of heart instead of pearl with ribbon trim. ∎

SOURCES: Paper paints from Plaid; PeelnStick double-sided adhesive sheets from Therm O Web; Gem-Tac adhesive from Beacon.

Baby Buggy Gift Set

Designs by SANDY ROLLINGER

MATERIALS
- 10 x 12-inch vellum gift bag
- 5 x 7-inch white card with envelope
- White vellum
- Dark pink and pink papers
- Pink patterned paper
- Self-adhesive baby sentiment stickers
- Small flower punch
- Decorative border punch
- 1-inch circle punch
- 1-inch flower punch
- ½-inch flower punch
- White and light pink paper paints
- 1/16-inch-wide white quilling paper strips
- Slotted quilling tool
- ¼-inch-wide pink satin ribbon
- Decorative-edge scissors
- Paper trimmer
- Instant-dry paper adhesive
- Double-sided adhesive sheets
- Adhesive foam squares

This set has many pretty embellishments including heart-shaped buttons, pearl trim and quilled accents.

DIAGRAMS ON PAGE 74

Gift Bag

Cut a 7 x 7½-inch piece of dark pink paper; use border punch to punch paper once on all four sides. Cut another piece from dark pink paper measuring 4½ inches square. Punch sides with border punch.

Cut a 5½-inch square from pink paper with decorative-edge scissors. Place dots of white paper paint along edges; let dry. Beginning with smallest piece of paper, layer and adhere papers on top of each other. Adhere layered piece to bag.

Trace baby buggy pattern onto pink patterned paper and cut out. Use 1-inch circle punch to make two circles from white card stock; punch out eight white flowers with the ¼-inch flower punch. Punch out six flowers from dark pink paper with the medium flower punch; punch out four white flowers with the large flower punch. Set aside.

Use patterns to form the quilling shapes as directed. Quill six white teardrop shapes from 3-inch-long quilling strips; adhere two teardrops together with paper adhesive to form a heart shape. Repeat with remaining teardrops. Quill an S scroll from a 4-inch-long quilling strip; quill two C scrolls from 4-inch-long quilling strips and quill one S scroll with one end left open for buggy handle.

Glue one flat quilling strip to the top edge of the buggy; glue another approximately 1 inch down from the first strip. Glue one additional quilling strip onto "bonnet" of buggy. Referring to photo for placement, begin gluing pieces in place. Glue two tiny white flowers onto the bonnet with the quilled S scroll between them; glue the three quilled hearts to the center of the buggy and a tiny white heart between each. Add foam squares to back of buggy and attach to bag. Glue handle to front of buggy; glue C scrolls to bottom of buggy. Attach white circles beside C scrolls as wheels; glue a medium pink flower to each wheel and then glue a tiny white flower on top. Finish buggy by applying a dot of white paint to the center of each flower.

Punch out four white flowers using large flower punch; punch out four dark pink flowers using medium flower punch. Adhere a pink flower on top of a white flower and apply a dot of white paper paint to center. Repeat for three additional flowers; adhere one to each corner of bag.

For gift tag, cut a 3½ x 10-inch piece of white card stock. Fold piece in half. Cut pink patterned paper 3 x 4½ inches using decorative-edge scissors. Cut dark pink paper 2 x 3 inches; trim edges with decorative-edge scissors. Apply baby stickers to dark pink paper; punch out two flowers using paper punches and adhere to tag. Add dots of paper paint to tag. Adhere word rectangle angled onto pink patterned paper and attach to white card. Use small flower punch to create a hole at top left corner of tag; insert ribbon through hole and tie to bag handle.

Card

Follow instructions for making bag, but use one 4½ x 6½-inch pink patterned paper rectangle and one 4 x 5-inch vellum rectangle for the background instead of three layered pieces. ■

SOURCES: Paper-Tac adhesive from Beacon; PeelnStick double-sided adhesive sheets from Therm O Web; paper paints from Plaid.

Fish Gift Bag

Design by SUSAN STRINGFELLOW

Catch the heart of a fisherman with a gift hidden inside this fun bag that's embellished with a bobber and fibers.

Cut a 3½ x 4½-inch piece of golden tan card stock; dampen card stock and crumple up. Dry in microwave for 30 seconds or let air-dry. **Note:** *Do not leave paper unattended while heating in microwave.* Attach two square gold eyelets in top corners of card stock.

Stamp the fish image onto off-white card stock; cut out and tear the right edge. Apply walnut ink to image; let dry. Cover the fish image with two layers of clear-drying dimensional adhesive and let dry. Attach to crumpled card stock.

Cut a ¾ x 4½-inch piece of mesh; attach to bottom of fish. Thread several fibers through eyelets and tie in a knot. Attach mini fishing ornaments from left eyelet. Adhere assembled piece to front of bag.

SOURCES: Mesh from Magic Mesh; Stampa Rosa rubber stamp from Creative Beginnings; Diamond Glaze cimensional adhesive from JudiKins; eyelets from Bag Works.

MATERIALS

Green gift bag
Off-white and golden tan card stock
Adhesive natural mesh
Fish rubber stamp
Brown ink pad
Walnut ink
Fishing-themed mini ornaments
2 square gold eyelets
Green and gold fibers
Clear-drying dimensional adhesive
Microwave (optional)

Masculine Gift Bag

Design by SANDY ROLLINGER

Create a special bag without frills or fuss for your next gift to a special man.

Cut a 5½ x 7½-inch piece of upholstery fabric; center and glue to bag with fabric adhesive. Cut a 4 x 5-inch rectangle from golden tan card stock; center and glue to bag with paper adhesive. Use a computer or hand-print desired name onto brown card stock; cut a 2½ x 3-inch rectangle around name; adhere toward top of golden tan card stock on bag.

Glue one of the fibers around the perimeter of the upholstery fabric; glue two other fibers around the perimeter of the golden tan rectangle. Repeat process with another fiber around the name rectangle; let all pieces dry. Gather several 3½-inch pieces of fibers together and tie one end to form a tassel. Thread large button with one piece of fiber and tie button onto fiber tassel. Adhere fibers underneath name rectangle with fabric adhesive.

For tag, use a computer or hand-print desired message onto golden tan card stock. Cut a 3 x 6-inch rectangle around message; score and fold in half to form a gift tag. Cut a 1 x 3-inch strip of brown card stock; cut a ½ x 3-inch strip of upholstery fabric. Layer fabric strip to brown strip; adhere a piece of fiber onto layered strips. Glue a small button onto strips; adhere to bottom of tag. Punch a hole at corner; thread a few fibers through hole and tie to bag handle. ■

SOURCES: Paper-Tac and Fabri-Tac adhesives from Beacon.

MATERIALS

- 8 x 10-inch brown corrugated gift bag
- Brown and golden tan card stock
- Brown and tan upholstery fabric pieces
- Yellow and gold fibers
- Brown buttons: 1 large and 1 small
- Instant-dry paper adhesive
- Fabric adhesive
- Ruler
- Hole punch
- Craft knife
- Computer font (optional)

The Great Outdoors Set

Designs by SANDRA GRAHAM SMITH

MATERIALS
- 8 x 10-inch brown bag with handles
- Forest-print paper
- Dark green and white card stock
- 4⅝ x 5¾-inch white envelope
- Vellum travel sentiments
- 2 copper eyelets
- Eyelet setting tool
- Small maple leaf punch
- Pine tree die-cut
- Die-cut machine
- 6 inches copper wire
- White gel pen
- Hole punch
- Ruler
- Stylus
- Glue stick

Die-cuts and wire accents add a distinctive touch to this nature-inspired gift set. DIAGRAMS ON PAGE 77

Gift Bag

Trace the bag collar pattern used for the School Days Gift Set onto forest-print paper; cut out. Fold collar in half on dotted line and cut out circles and line. Use die-cut machine and pine tree die-cut to cut one pine tree from forest-print paper; cut three pine trees from dark green card stock. Glue two dark green trees to the lower left corner of bag; glue forest-print tree overlapping dark green trees.

Put collar on top of bag. Punch a hole on top of remaining pine tree; thread copper wire through hole. Twist wire around bag handle; wrap wire around itself several times to secure. Wrap wire ends around a pencil to curl. Write "to" and "from" on tree tag with gel pen.

Card with Envelope

Cut white card stock 5½ x 8½ inches; score and fold in half. Cut a 4 x 5¼-inch piece of forest-print paper; adhere to card. Use die-cut machine and pine tree die-cut to cut one pine tree from dark green card stock. Glue pine tree to white card stock; cut out leaving a small border. Center and glue to card. Carefully tear out desired vellum travel sentiment; attach to card at an angle with copper eyelets.

For envelope, cut one pine tree from dark green card stock; cut another pine tree from forest-print paper. Glue trees to envelope overlapping each other; trim tree trunks.

Cut a 1¼-inch square of forest-print paper; punch a maple leaf in center of square and adhere to envelope flap. ■

SOURCES: Forest-print paper from NRN Designs; Deja Views vellum sentiment from The C-Thru Ruler Co.

Party-Time Set

Design by KATHLEEN PANEITZ

MATERIALS
- Orange and green patterned papers
- Coordinating striped paper
- Coordinating alphabet stickers
- Off-white, yellow and pink card stock
- Bag die-cut
- Tiny flower and birthday cupcake rubber stamps
- Dark pink and pink ink pads
- Buttons
- Pink ribbon
- "Partytime" word embellishment
- Purple curling ribbon
- Thin pink wire-edged ribbon
- Birthday package square charm
- Sewing needle
- Lime green embroidery floss
- Sewing machine with orange sewing thread
- Orange teardrop jewel
- Chalks
- Clear dimensional adhesive
- Double-sided tape
- Ultra-fine pink glitter
- Pink flower eyelet
- 2 pink eyelets
- Party blower

Make your gift the talk of the party by enclosing it in this eye-catching set!

Birthday Bag

Use bag die-cut to cut birthday bag from yellow card stock. Determine bag front and use a zigzag stitch to machine-sew a small striped paper rectangle toward bottom of bag. Also machine-stitch a rounded piece of striped paper onto bag closure flap. Trim edges if needed.

Attach two pink eyelets in middle of striped rectangle; thread purple curling ribbon through eyelets and tie on a party blower. Adhere alphabet stickers vertically on bag to spell "Party On"; tie a piece of pink ribbon around closure flap. Secure ribbon with double-sided tape. Adhere desired buttons; assemble bag.

Birthday Tag

Cut a 4¾ x 2¾-inch rectangle from pink card stock; cut top two corners diagonally to form a tag shape. Stamp the tiny flower image over entire surface with dark pink ink; let dry. Tear a piece of orange patterned paper and adhere at top of tag; trim edges. Adhere another piece of orange patterned paper across center of tag; trim edges and use sewing needle and lime green thread to stitch paper to tag.

Adhere "Partytime" embellishment toward top of tag. Use dark pink ink to stamp birthday cupcake image onto off-white card stock; let dry. Color in image with chalks. Apply a thin layer of clear dimensional adhesive to cupcake frosting and sprinkle on a small amount of ultra-fine glitter; let dry.

Apply clear dimensional adhesive to rest of cupcake to add dimension; let dry. Adhere teardrop jewel to candle for flame. Cut a rectangle around image and apply pink ink to edges; adhere to tag. Thread thin wired pink ribbon through birthday package charm; tie a bow and adhere to tag.

Cut a small rectangle from green patterned paper and apply pink ink to edges. Adhere rectangle at top of tag; insert pink flower eyelet through center of rectangle. Apply pink ink to tag edges. ■

SOURCES: Patterned papers from KI Memories; rubber stamps from Hero Arts and Stampabilities; birthday charm, alphabet stickers and striped paper from Doodlebug Design Inc.; Crystal Effects from Stampin' Up!; bag die-cut from AccuCut.

BAGS

⊣ BAGS ⊢

Glamour Girl Set
Designs by SANDRA GRAHAM SMITH

MATERIALS
Makeup-print paper
Makeup-themed stickers
White, hot pink and bright green card stock
3⅝ x 5⅛-inch white envelope
Decorative-edge scissors
Adhesive foam dots
Ruler

Treat your favorite diva to a fashion-inspired gift nestled in this tiny package. Pretty makeup-themed paper makes creating a coordinating card simple. DIAGRAMS ON PAGE 74

Gift Box

Glue a sheet of makeup-print paper to white card stock. Use box pattern used for the Patriotic Gift Set and trace onto layered card stock; use a ruler and stylus to score dashed lines. Cut out box; cut inside handles with a craft knife. Assemble box and glue tab.

Mount two makeup-themed stickers to white card stock; cut out and attach to front of box with adhesive foam dots.

Card with Envelope

Cut white card stock 5 x 7 inches; score and fold in half. Cut a 5 x 7-inch piece of makeup-print paper; measure ½ inch in from each edge and cut out a rectangle opening with decorative-edge scissors. Adhere to card.

Cut two 1⅜-inch squares from hot pink card stock; use decorative-edge scissors to cut two 1¾-inch squares from bright green card stock. Layer pink squares on top of green squares and adhere to center of card. Attach several makeup-themed stickers to layered squares.

For envelope, place stickers randomly on front and back flap. ■

SOURCES: Patterned paper from Colors by Design; stickers from Stickopotamus/EK Success; box pattern from AccuCut.

Beaded Gift Bag
Design by LAURIE D'AMBROSIC

Embellish a gift bag with your favorite colors of beads and trims!

Stamp flower image onto light purple card stock using purple ink; let dry. Use flower template to add leaves and tendrils with green colored pencil. Wrap the nonstick cloth around the plate of the iron so that the adhesive in the iron-on ribbon and braid do not stick to the iron. Following manufacturer's instructions, attach iron-on ribbon around flower edge and in the flower's center. Attach braiding around leaves and tendrils. Carefully tear a square around flower; attach to bag with adhesive dots.

Cut a 6-inch length of beaded fringe trim; fold over the ends ½ inch and secure with an adhesive dot. Attach the trim to the top edge of bag with double-sided tape. Make sure to secure threads on back of trim so beads will not fall off.

For tag, cut a 2 x 4-inch piece of light purple card stock; score and fold in half. Punch a square hole in the corner; cut a slit from the corner to the hole. Attach card to bag.

SOURCES: Foam stamp and template from Loew-Cornell; iron-on ribbon, iron-on braid, Teflon cloth and mini iron from Kreinik; beaded fringe trim from Hirschberg Schutz & Co

MATERIALS
- 5 x 8-inch light blue paper bag
- Light purple card stock
- Flower sponge stamp and matching flower template
- Purple ink pad
- Green colored pencil
- Beaded flower fringe trim
- Pink iron-on ribbon
- Green iron-on braid
- Nonstick cloth
- Mini iron
- Double-sided tape
- Adhesive dots
- ¼-inch square punch

Patriotic Gift Set

Designs by SANDRA GRAHAM SMITH

MATERIALS
Red card stock
Red and blue star patterned paper
3⅝ x 5⅛-inch white envelope
5 x 7-inch white card stock
Small box template
Medium and small star punches
5 gold star brads
Ruler
Stylus
Glue stick
Craft knife
Adhesive foam dots

Show your patriotic pride with this star-studded set! Gold star brads add shine to this set. DIAGRAMS ON PAGE 74

Gift Box

Use small box template to trace a box onto red card stock; use a ruler and stylus to score the dashed lines. Cut out box; cut inside handles with a craft knife. Assemble box and glue tab.

Trace star pattern onto blue star patterned paper; cut out and attach to box with an adhesive foam dot. Use medium star punch to punch out two stars from blue patterned paper and one star from red patterned paper. Insert a star brad through the center of both blue stars and attach to handle. Attach a star brad to the center of the red star; attach star to large blue star on box with an adhesive foam dot.

Card with Envelope

Score and fold white card stock in half. Cut two ½ x 5-inch strips of red star patterned paper; cut a strip from blue star patterned paper the same size. Referring to photo, weave strips together and adhere to front of card. Trim edges if needed.

Trace two large stars onto blue patterned paper; cut out and glue to card. Punch two stars from red star patterned paper with medium star punch; attach a star brad through center of each red star and adhere to blue stars on card with foam dots.

For envelope, cut a ½ x 3⅝-inch strip of red star patterned paper; adhere to left side of envelope. Trace large star onto blue patterned paper; cut out and glue to envelope. Use medium star punch to make two stars from red paper and one star from blue paper. Glue one red star onto the large blue star. Glue remaining red star next to large star; glue medium blue star to envelope flap.

With small star punch, make two stars from blue paper and one star from red paper. Glue stars to front and back of envelope. ■

SOURCES: Patterned papers from DieCuts with a View; box pattern from AccuCut.

"Pour Vous" Gift Bag

Design by SUSAN STRINGFELLOW

French influence is everywhere; showcase your next gift in this pretty and stylish bag!

Cut a piece of brown kraft paper large enough to wrap around the gift box; crumple up the paper. Gently unfold and iron just enough to flatten. Wrap the box with the crumpled paper leaving one end completely open; slip box out of wrapping and fold open ends inside. Rub the surface of the bag with brown and black ink pads.

Punch two holes on the front and back. Cut two 10-inch lengths of ribbon; dip ribbon into walnut ink and allow to dry. Insert into holes and tie knots to secure.

Attach a vintage image and postage stamp sticker to front of bag; use black acrylic paint to stamp the decorative corner image over the left edge of vintage image. Lightly sponge cream paint onto the image and stamp again onto the black. Stamp "pour vous mon ami" (for you my friend) in the upper right corner of bag with alphabet stamps. Attach several coordinating silk flowers to bag using mini brads. ■

SOURCES: Decorative corner foam stamp and mini brads from Making Memories; vintage image from Altered Pages; sticker from Me & My Big Ideas; alphabet rubber stamps from Hero Arts; solvent-based ink pad from Tsukineko.

MATERIALS

- Small gift box
- Kraft paper
- Black and white striped ribbon
- Vintage French image
- Postage stamp sticker
- Small silk flowers
- Decorative corner foam stamp
- Small alphabet stamps
- Black and cream acrylic paints
- Foam brush
- Solvent-based black ink pad
- Brown ink pad
- Walnut ink
- Antiqued mini brads
- Iron
- Glue stick

BAGS

Paper Leaves Gift Set

Design by KATHY WEGNER

MATERIALS
- 8¼ x 5¼-inch corrugated Kraft bag with handles
- 5½ x 4-inch corrugated Kraft note card with envelope
- Tan, golden yellow and rust card stock
- 3 x 4-inch pieces Kraft paper and corrugated Kraft paper
- Transfer paper
- Tan, golden yellow and rust ink pads
- Brown eyelash yarn
- Brown embroidery floss
- Paper adhesive
- Sponge-tip applicators
- Bone folder
- Soft surface, such as thick craft foam or a mouse pad
- ⅛-inch hole punch

Corrugated cardboard adds texture to this autumn-inspired set. DIAGRAMS ON PAGE 75

Use leaf patterns provided to cut one small leaf and one large leaf from golden yellow card stock; cut two large leaves each from rust and tan card stock. Place leaves on a soft surface; gently indent vein lines with bone folder. Erase any transfer lines that can be seen. Rub coordinating ink pad around edges of each leaf and over the veins; let dry.

Referring to photo, adhere eyelash yarn up one side of bag front; wrap yarn around handle and adhere down other side of bag. Repeat for reverse side. Adhere eyelash yarn to top of note card along with a large tan and a large rust leaf; adhere remaining large leaves to bag.

For gift card, fold 3 x 4-inch pieces of Kraft paper and Kraft corrugated paper in half. Place Kraft paper inside corrugated paper; trim off excess. Adhere papers together and attach a piece of eyelash yarn across top of tag; adhere small leaf to tag. Punch a hole in corner and tie to handle with embroidery floss. ■

Teacher Gift Bag

Design by HELEN RAFSON

Add homemade cookies and other goodies to this bag, and you'll have an inexpensive gift that your child's teacher will love! DIAGRAMS ON PAGE 75

Fold top section of bag over to form a flap; draw stitch lines onto flap and around edges of bag with black marker. Trace apple pattern onto red patterned paper; trace leaf pattern onto green patterned paper and trace stem pattern onto brown card stock. Cut out apple and stem; cut out leaves with pinking shears. Draw stitch lines around apple and leaves; draw a solid line around stem.

Referring to photo for placement, adhere pieces to bag. Attach alphabet stickers toward bottom of bag. Glue on buttons with gem adhesive; let dry. Punch two ¼-inch holes at bag flap. Fill bag with treats; insert ribbon through holes and tie into a bow.

For tag, cut a 1⅝ x 1⅞-inch piece of black card stock. Draw stitch lines around perimeter and write teacher's name onto tag with white gel pen. Punch a hole at top of tag with ⅛-inch hole punch; punch same size hole at top corner of bag. Insert white ribbon through holes in tag and bag; tie into a knot. ■

SOURCES: Ruler-print ribbon from Offray; Gem-Tac and Kid's Choice Glue from Beacon.

MATERIALS

- Brown paper bag
- Red and green patterned papers
- Brown and black card stock
- Tracing paper
- Black letter stickers
- 3 tan buttons
- Green button
- 20½ inches ruler-print ribbon
- 6 inches ⅛-inch-wide white satin ribbon
- Black fine-tip permanent marker
- White gel pen
- Ruler
- Pinking shears
- ¼- and ⅛-inch hole punches
- Gem adhesive
- Instant-hold glue

School Days Gift Set

Designs by SANDRA GRAHAM SMITH

MATERIALS
- 8 x 10-inch brown paper bag with handles
- 5½ x 8½-inch white card stock
- 4⅝ x 5¾-inch white envelope
- Chalkboard-print paper
- School patchwork–print paper
- Red raffia
- Black permanent marker
- Small hole punch
- Ruler
- Stylus
- Glue stick

School-themed paper makes it easy to create a coordinating gift set ideal for a back-to-school treat.

DIAGRAMS ON PAGE 76

Gift Bag

Trace bag collar pattern onto school patchwork–print paper; cut out. Fold collar in half on dotted line and cut out circles and along line. Trace apple pattern onto school patchwork–print paper; cut out and glue to bottom right corner of bag. Trace leaf pattern onto chalkboard-print paper; cut out and glue above apple. Trace "A," "B" and "C" onto the reverse side of the chalkboard-print paper. ***Note:*** *The patterns are reversed so that when they are traced onto the back of the printed paper, they will be correct when turned over. Glue letters onto the left portion of bag. With black marker, draw a stem above paper apple.*

For tag, cut a 2½ x 5-inch piece of chalkboard-print paper; fold in half and punch a hole in one corner. Write "to" and "from" inside card. Put collar on top of bag; thread raffia through gift tag and tie to front handle.

Card and Envelope

Score and fold white card stock in half. Cut a 4¼ x 5½-inch piece of chalkboard-print paper; glue to card front. Cut a 1 x 5½-inch strip from school patchwork–print paper; glue to left edge of card and trim edges.

Trace "A," "B" and "C" onto the reverse side of school patchwork–print paper; cut out and glue to card front. Trim edges even.

For envelope, cut a 1⅛ x 5¾-inch strip of school patchwork–print paper; adhere to bottom of envelope and trim edges. Cut one patchwork square from paper; glue to envelope flap. ■

SOURCES: Printed papers from Provo Craft.

Get Ready for Treats!

Designs by ANNIE LANG

MATERIALS
- 2½ sheets 9 x 12-inch 140-pound watercolor paper
- 13 x 10-inch black paper bag with handles
- 7¾ x 11-inch bright green card stock
- Transfer paper
- Black extra-fine-and medium-tip permanent marking pens
- Acrylic paints: white, light yellow, antique gold, red, light peach, dark green, bright green, black, turquoise, purple, blush, orange and periwinkle
- Assorted paintbrushes
- Matte-finish spray sealer
- Palette
- Water container
- Adhesive sheets
- Adhesive dots

Ghosts and goblins of all ages will be excited to attend your next Halloween party when they receive this whimsical coordinating invitation and treat bag set.

DIAGRAMS ON PAGE 78

Treat Bag

Enlarge pattern and transfer to center of watercolor paper; paint as directed.

Girl's face and hands: Paint with peach; when dry, highlight desired areas with blush paint thinned with a small amount of water. Use a round brush to apply thinned red paint onto cheek areas. Paint nose blush and tongue peach; paint inner mouth black. With a liner brush, add tiny white highlight dots to cheeks and nose.

Dress: Highlight desired areas on top section with thinned turquoise paint; paint middle section light yellow and then highlight with antique gold. Paint bottom section orange; highlight with red. Nose and tongue are painted orange and inner mouth black. Paint cheeks as directed for girl; add white highlight dots to nose and cheeks.

Shoes: Paint bright green; highlight edges with dark green. When dry, use a liner brush to add a few white highlight lines to each.

Hair: Paint light yellow; highlight with antique gold.

Ghost hat: Highlight edges with turquoise; paint cheeks as directed for girl's face. Paint nose orange; paint inner mouth black with white tongue; paint hat strap black. When dry, use liner brush to add white highlight lines to hat strap.

Pumpkin: Paint orange; highlight desired areas with red. Fill in eye and inner mouth area with black paint. Tongue remains orange and nose is painted red; paint cheeks and add highlights as directed for girl's face.

Spider: Paint black; use a liner brush to add white smile and highlights. Paint eyes and string bright green and highlight desired areas with dark green.

Bats: In unused margins of watercolor paper, transfer patterns for five bats. Thin black paint with water to create a dark gray wash; paint bats with mixture. When dry, highlight a small amount of thinned black around wing lines; paint bows and eyes bright green. When bats are dry, flip watercolor paper over and paint back of paper black.

Background: Highlight around all outlines with periwinkle. Thin paint with water to create a wash; apply color onto background using a back-and-forth "flipping" motion. Carefully use a medium-point black marker and ruler to add the black frame that separates border from background.

Border: Paint border with periwinkle. When dry, highlight areas that overlap into border with purple paint.

Add outlining and remaining details with extra-fine-tip marking pen.

Lightly mist all painted objects with two or three coats of sealer, letting pieces dry between coats.

Once painting is completely dry, turn design over; locate middle face section on pumpkin and mark it. Adhesive will not be applied to this area so a treat can be tucked inside.

Apply double-sided adhesive to back of design, cutting sheet into strips as necessary to avoid applying them to the pumpkin pocket. Do not remove paper backing yet.

Cut out painting from paper. Using a craft knife, cut a slit along indicated line on large pumpkin.

Remove protective paper backing from adhesive on back of design; attach to front of bag and press firmly into place.

Cut out bats and bend wings forward. Apply adhesive to middle section of bat; attach all bats to bag, using photo as guide.

Invitation

Transfer pattern as shown to watercolor paper and paint as directed for larger painting. Transfer bat pattern to watercolor paper; paint as directed previously.

Fold card stock in half. Apply double-sided adhesive to back of painted design; attach to front of card. Open card and cut a slit along indicated line on pumpkin, wide enough to insert a small lollipop.

Cut out bat and bend wings forward. Attach adhesive to middle section of bat and adhere to card, referring to photo for placement. ■

SOURCES: Acrylic paint and matte-finish spray sealer from DecoArt.

Gingerbread Gift Bags

Designs by HELEN RAFSON

MATERIALS
- Brown Kraft gift bags
- White and brown corrugated paper
- Red card stock
- Red and green dotted paper
- White poster board
- Tracing paper
- ¼- and ⅛-inch hole punches
- Heart punch
- White baby rickrack
- Black florist wire
- 8 (6mm) half round black balls
- 7mm alphabet beads
- White acrylic paint
- Black fine-tip permanent marker
- White embroidery floss
- 7⅜ inches ¼-inch-wide gold ribbon
- 10 inches ⅛-inch-wide red and green satin ribbon
- 8 white eyelets
- Eyelet setting tool
- Instant-dry paper adhesive
- Instant-hold glue
- Toothpick
- Sewing needle
- Ruler
- Decorative-edge scissors

The small size of these bags is ideal for fresh-baked holiday goodies or small gifts. DIAGRAMS ON PAGE 79

Cut a 4 x 6-inch piece of red or green dotted paper; attach eyelets in each corner with a ⅛-inch hole punch. Center and adhere to bag. Glue white rickrack around edges of paper; let dry. Punch four hearts from red card stock; draw tiny stitch lines onto hearts with permanent marker. Adhere hearts to corners of bag.

Trace patterns to back of corrugated paper as indicated; cut out. If making gingerbread girl, cut out bottom of apron with decorative-edge scissors and punch ⅛-inch holes along apron edge. Referring to photo, glue rickrack onto gingerbread boy or girl. Cut a 1-inch piece of black florist wire; bend into a U shape and glue onto gingerbread boy or girl for mouth. Glue on two half round black balls for eyes. For girl, punch out four hearts from red card stock; punch out two hearts for boy. Dip end of toothpick into white paint and make highlights onto hearts; let dry. Glue on hearts, referring to photo for placement. For boy, punch three circles from red card stock and glue on as buttons. Tie a bow with gold ribbon; trim ends and glue onto gingerbread boy or girl. Adhere to bag.

For the tag, glue white rickrack around dotted paper heart and let dry. Glue paper heart to the front of the white poster board heart. Punch two hearts from red card stock. Bend a ¾-inch piece of black florist wire into a slight curve; glue hearts onto ends of wire and let dry. Glue assembled wire and two half round black balls onto gingerbread head as the facial features.

Cut two ½-inch-diameter circles from brown corrugated paper; glue onto decorated heart as hands and let dry. Thread sewing needle with embroidery floss and insert into left side of heart; thread on alphabet beads spelling desired name. Insert needle through to the back; knot floss and glue ends to secure. Glue matching heart to back to cover floss; let dry.

Glue head onto heart. Punch a ⅛-inch hole at top of tag; insert ribbon through hole and tie onto bag. Trim ends. ■

SOURCES: Dotted paper and brown paper bag from Hot Off The Press; Kid's Choice Glue and Paper-Tac adhesives from Beacon; corrugated paper from DMD Inc.

BAGS

Snowman Gift Bag

Design by HELEN RAFSON

Eye-catching metallic garland adds a festive touch and gives pizzazz to this seasonal bag. DRAWINGS ON PAGE 79

Trace patterns onto indicated corrugated paper; cut out. Glue hatband onto hat; let dry. Punch two ¼-inch circles from black card stock; punch two hearts from red card stock. Dip end of toothpick into white paint and place a dot on the center of black circles and hearts; let dry.

Cut fourteen ¾-inch lengths of red embroidery floss; glue seven floss pieces to the reverse side of one of the scarf ends; trim ends even. Separate strands with a sewing pin. Glue remaining floss pieces to other scarf end.

Cut a piece of red embroidery floss and insert into sewing needle; thread red button and tie a knot at top. Trim ends. Glue button onto scarf with gem adhesive; let dry. Referring to photo for placement, assemble and adhere snowman to bag.

Cut a 1-inch-long piece of black embroidery floss. Glue piece onto snowman's face as his mouth; glue punched circles, hearts and orange pompom as his remaining facial features. Cut a 5¼-inch piece of silver rickrack; glue toward bottom of bag. Glue four snowflakes to bag; adhere rhinestones to snowflakes and then randomly onto bag. Cut two 11-inch pieces of silver star garland; wrap garland around handles twisting ends around handle to secure.

For tag, cut a 1½-inch square from white card stock with decorative-edge scissors. Punch a ⅛-inch hole in each corner; adhere snowflake onto center of tag. Attach a rhinestone to snowflake. Draw stitch lines around edges and perimeter of snowflake. Thread white ribbon through hole; tie onto bag. ■

SOURCES: Corrugated paper and gift bag from DMD Inc.; Gem-Tac and Kid's Choice adhesives from Beacon; silver snowflakes from Nicole Crafts.

MATERIALS

- Light blue gift bag
- White, red and black corrugated paper
- White, red and black card stock
- Tracing paper
- White acrylic paint
- Red and black embroidery floss
- Red button
- 2 blue buttons
- 5mm orange pompom
- 5 silver snowflakes
- 11 (7mm) clear rhinestones
- Silver star garland
- 6 inches ⅛-inch-wide white satin ribbon
- Silver rickrack
- Black fine-tip permanent marker
- ¼- and ⅛-inch hole punches
- Heart punch
- Sewing pin
- Sewing needle
- Decorative-edge scissors
- Instant-hold glue
- Gem adhesive
- Toothpick

Snowman Set

Design by COLLEEN RUNDGREN
for American Traditional Designs

Use rub-on transfers to create a gift set that is quick and easy to complete. These adorable snowmen are charming additions to any winter gifts.

Snowman Tag

Lightly draw a 2⅞-inch diameter circle onto the back of snowflake patterned paper; add a small half circle at top. Cut out and adhere to white card stock with patterned side face up. Trim perimeter of tag leaving a narrow white border. Adhere a torn piece of white card stock to lower edge of tag; trim edges.

Transfer a snowman rub-on to white card stock; cut out image. Adhere to green card stock; trim edges leaving a small border. Center and attach to tag with adhesive foam dots. Punch a hole at top and loop ribbon through.

Snowman Gift Bag

Remove handles from gift bag; adhere snowflake patterned paper to the entire outside surface of bag. Attach alphabet stickers to white card stock to spell "Let It Snow"; cut letters into squares and attach to bottom front of bag. Attach some letters with glue stick and others with adhesive foam dots.

Cut 8 x 8-inch squares of dark blue card stock and ice skates patterned paper; adhere papers together. Trim corners into rounded shapes and fold in half creating a flap. Punch holes along the crease approximately 1 inch from each side edge; string shoelaces through holes and knot to create a handle. Glue the back half of flap to the inside back of bag. Attach hook and loop circles under flap to create a closure.

Make another snowman tag as directed above, only instead of attaching with ribbon use swirl clip to attach tag to shoelace handle. ■

SOURCES: Rub-on transfers, alphabet stickers, patterned papers and swirl clip from American Traditional Designs.

MATERIALS
Snowflake patterned paper
Green striped paper
Red and white card stock
Green and brown corrugated papers
Small snowman and small tree rubber stamps
Black ink pad
Gold star brads
3 x 3-inch reclosable plastic bags
Colored pencils
Small hole punch
Small snowflake punch
Decorative-edge scissors
Glue stick
Ruler
Stylus
Candy

Santa Set

Design by COLLEEN RUNDGREN *for American Traditional Designs*

Let your loved ones know they've been nice this year with a gift packaged in this cute coordinating set.

Santa Tag

Lightly trace tag onto snowflake patterned paper; measure and cut snowflake paper ⅛ inch smaller. Center and adhere to tag. Punch a hole in patterned paper to match tag hole. Transfer a Santa rub-on to white card stock; cut out image. Center and adhere to tag with adhesive foam dots. Loop red ribbon through hole.

Santa Gift Bag

Adhere green Christmas patterned paper to entire outside surface of bag. Create another tag as directed above. Center and adhere blue ribbon around bag overlapping ends in back. Attach gold Christmas clip to ribbon; insert tag into clip. Secure tag with adhesive.

SOURCES: Rub-on transfers, patterned papers and gold Christmas clip from American Traditional Designs.

MATERIALS

- 2 Santa rub-on transfers
- 2 (2¾ x 3½-inch) white tags
- Snowflake patterned paper
- 2 sheets green Christmas patterned paper
- White card stock
- ⅓ yard narrow red ribbon
- ½ yard narrow blue ribbon
- Gold Christmas clip
- Small gift bag
- Adhesive foam dots
- Hole punch
- Glue stick
- Craft glue

⊣ BAGS ⊢

Tiny Treats Bags

Design by SANDRA GRAHAM SMITH

Stuff your family's stockings with their favorite candy packaged in handmade treat bags. Individualize each bag with your favorite holiday stamps. DIAGRAMS ON PAGE 80

Trace bag pattern onto red card stock and cut out; cut out center circle with decorative-edge scissors. Score and fold dashed lines. Punch out two snowflakes on bag at dots indicated on pattern.

Stamp tree image onto white card stock; color in design and cut out with decorative-edge scissors. Layer image onto a 1½-inch green corrugated paper square; layer again onto a 1¾-inch green striped paper square. Adhere assembled piece to what will be the bottom left corner of bag when assembled.

Fill reclosable plastic bag with candy and place in the middle of card stock bag; fold bag up and fasten with two star brads attached in both upper corners.

For snowflake bag, follow same directions as above, but use snowflake patterned paper instead of red card stock. Stamp snowman image and layer onto brown corrugated paper and red card stock. ■

SOURCES: Rubber stamps from Stampin' Up!; patterned paper from Hot Off The Press.

MATERIALS
Snowflake patterned paper
Green striped paper
Red and white card stock
Green and brown corrugated papers
Small snowman and small tree rubber stamps
Black ink pad
Gold star brads
3 x 3-inch reclosable plastic bags
Colored pencils
Small hole punch
Small snowflake punch
Decorative-edge scissors
Glue stick
Ruler
Stylus
Candy

⊣ BAGS ⊢

Spirelli Christmas Series
Designs by MARILYNNE OSKAMP

MATERIALS
- Small and medium Spirelli star punches
- Paper weaving punch
- Small star hole punch
- Star border stencil
- Red and cream lightweight card stock
- Red and cream heavyweight card stock
- Cream card
- 5-inch square red envelope
- Red and gold star-print foil paper
- Small gold circle stickers
- Small gold star sticker
- 2mm adhesive foam tape
- 3mm adhesive foam squares
- Red and gold metallic thread
- Metallic gold ribbon
- Double-sided tape
- Medium embossing tool
- Cellophane tape
- Ruler
- Craft knife
- Computer font (optional)

These projects look complicated, but special punches make quick work of cutting out the intricate shapes. Wrapping with gold thread is easy! DIAGRAMS ON PAGE 81

Project note: When winding thread around the Spirelli stars, first tape the end of the thread to the reverse side. Bring the thread around to the front and skip the number of points indicated in instructions. Diagram shows eight points being skipped. Wind the thread around to the back of the star coming up again between the points to the right of where thread began. Cross thread over existing thread and go down between the points to the left of the last thread. Continue in this fashion until pattern is completed. When finished, secure ends with tape. Refer to Spirelli diagram throughout.

Merry Christmas Card

Enlarge folded card pattern 125 percent; use pattern to cut card from lightweight red card stock. Emboss the fold lines with a ruler and embossing tool. Use a computer or hand-print message onto a 5-inch square cut from lightweight cream card stock. Punch out four small Spirelli stars from heavyweight cream card stock; punch out three stars from red foil.

Cut a ⅓ x 6-inch strip each of red and gold foil; use paper weaving punch to create weaving slits at the center of the bottom and right edges. Weave the red foil strip through bottom slits; weave gold foil strip through right edge slits. Wrap ends around to back and secure with cellophane tape. Attach square inside red card with double-sided tape.

Begin to wind the red and gold threads around the punched cream stars as directed. For two of the stars, use red metallic thread and skip ten points for the first layer. For the second layer, use gold metallic thread and skip eight points; for third layer use red metallic thread and skip six points.

For remaining stars, use gold metallic thread for first layer and skip ten points. For second layer, use red metallic thread and skip eight points; use gold metallic thread for third level and skip six points.

Glue foil stars in upper left corner of card; attach threaded stars offset of foil stars with adhesive foam tape and dots. Fold the red card closed and secure card with remaining star. Place card inside envelope.

Star Card

Punch two medium and two small stars from heavyweight red card stock; punch two medium and two small stars from gold foil. Wind gold thread around medium red stars skipping six points. Wind gold thread around small red stars skipping nine points. Punch weaving slits at bottom edge of card; cut a ⅓ x 6¼-inch strip of gold foil paper and insert through slits. Wrap ends inside card and secure with cellophane tape.

Dry emboss star border across top of card and above gold foil strip. Referring to photo for placement, glue the medium gold stars to card. Use double-sided tape to attach the threaded medium

BAGS

stars on top of gold foil stars; attach small gold foil stars on top of threaded stars and use adhesive foam tape to attach the small threaded stars on top of small gold foil stars.

Gift Tag

Punch one medium star from heavyweight cream card stock; set star aside and cut around punched star shape to form a tag. Punch one small star from heavyweight cream card stock and one small star from gold foil. Punch weaving slits into the bottom of the tag. Cut a small ⅓-inch-wide strip of gold foil and weave through slits; wrap ends around to back and secure with tape.

Layer tag onto red heavyweight card stock; trim edges leaving a small border. Place a small star sticker at top of tag; use small star punch to create a hole through sticker. Glue small gold foil star inside center opening of tag. Thread small cream star with red metallic thread, skipping ten points for the first layer. Use gold metallic thread for the second layer and skip eight points; use red metallic thread for the first layer and skip six points.

Attach threaded star on top of gold star with adhesive foam tape; thread gold ribbon through top of tag. Add small gold circle stickers between each point of punched-out star shape.

Red Gift Bag

Using Spirelli star punches, punch one medium and two small stars from heavyweight cream card stock; punch one medium and two small stars from gold foil. Wind thread around stars as directed. For the small stars, use red metallic thread for first layer and skip ten points. Use gold metallic thread for second layer skipping eight points; use red metallic thread for third layer skipping six points. For the medium stars, use red metallic thread and skip ten points. For second layer, use gold metallic thread and skip eight points; skip six points for third layer and use red metallic thread. Attach foil stars to bag; attach threaded stars on top of foil stars with adhesive foam tape. ■

SOURCES: Spirelli star punches, paper weaving punch, star border stencil, card stock, cream card, red and gold star-print foil, red square envelope, gold stickers, adhesive foam tape and foam squares and metallic threads from Ecstasy Crafts; star hole punch from Provo Craft.

⊣ BAGS ⊢

Stamped Bubble Mailer
Design by LAURIE D'AMBROSIO

Send gifts in style with stamped bubble envelopes. Use a variety of colors to personalize your mailer.

Use adhesive notes to mask off areas for the addresses and postage. ***Note:*** *The post office needs to have blank space around the address in order to deliver.* Crumple up a piece of plastic wrap; apply green ink to the plastic wrap and pounce it randomly on the front of the envelope. Repeat with another piece of plastic wrap and red ink. Once dry, remove adhesive notes.

MATERIALS
- White bubble envelope
- Green and red ink pads
- Plastic wrap
- Adhesive paper notes

BAGS

Winter Holidays Paper Purse

Design by SANDY ROLLINGER

MATERIALS
Off-white card stock
Decorative gold button
2 pearl cabochons
4 x 8mm oval white pearls
4mm gold beads
12 inches crystal bead fringe trim
12 inches off-white decorative trim
20-gauge gold wire
Needle-nose wire cutters
Heart rubber stamp
White embossing ink pad
Pearl embossing powder
Heat embossing tool
Hook-and-loop tape
¼-inch-wide double-sided tape
Bone folder
Instant-dry paper adhesive
Paper trimmer

A fancy beaded handle adds a trendy touch to a miniature handbag that's the right size for bridesmaids gifts at a winter wedding. DIAGRAMS ON PAGE 82

Use pattern provided to trace and cut out purse onto off-white card stock; use a paper trimmer to cut the straight edges. Score dashed lines. Lay purse flat on work surface and randomly stamp heart image onto the entire surface. Emboss with pearl embossing powder.

Cut a 10-inch length of gold wire; use needle-nose part of wire cutters to create a swirl at one end. Alternate stringing gold and pearl beads onto wire; curl remaining end into a swirl shape. Gently bend wire to form a handle.

Fold paper purse on scored lines. Cut two 1 x 4-inch strips of off-white card stock and fold accordion pleats lengthwise in each one. Apply double-sided tape to the two edges of each strip and place strips on each inside purse edge; press firmly to attach.

Adhere beaded fringe trim to the outside flap; let dry. Adhere off-white decorative trim onto flap covering fringe edge. Leave approximately ½ inch unglued at the top of each edge of purse flap; slip wire handle ends into these areas. Wrap trim ends over wire and glue trim onto back of purse to secure. Cover trim and fringe ends by adhering pearl cabochons. Glue gold and pearl button to the front flap center; glue a piece of hook-and-loop tape to the underside of flap. Let dry before opening. ■

SOURCES: Zip Dry paper adhesive from Beacon.

Elegant Snowflake Bag

Design by LAURIE D'AMBROSIO

Present your next gift in style with this pretty bag embellished with sparkling Austrian crystals.

Cut the border stickers to fit the length of the bag and attach one to each front edge. Center and place the snowflake sticker on bag. Use the heat-set rhinestone tool to attach stones to the top of the sticker; place smaller stones on the outer edges of the snowflake and place a larger rhinestone in the center.

For tag, cut a 2 x 4-inch piece of blue card stock; fold in half. Add border stickers on the side edges; center and attach a large rhinestone on front of tag. Punch a hole in upper corner; thread ribbon through tag and tie onto bag handle. ■

SOURCES: PSX stickers from Duncan; heat-set rhinestone tool and rhinestones from Creative Crystals Co.

MATERIALS

5 x 8-inch light purple gift bag
Dark blue card stock
Snowflake and coordinating border stickers
8 inches light purple organdy ribbon
Light sapphire and crystal heat-set rhinestones in assorted sizes
Heat-set rhinestone tool
1/8-inch hole punch

⊣ BAGS ⊢

Love Gift Bag
Design by LORETTA MATEIK

Hearts strung on wire add a stylish accent to this embellished bag. Personalize this design for any event by changing the phrase and color scheme.

Use the red dye ink pad to stamp Valentine sentiment onto metal-edge tag; cut a 1¾-inch circle from double-sided adhesive sheet and attach to tag. Punch out hole in tag and cover adhesive sheet with clear micro beads.

Use the red solvent-based ink pad to stamp six small hearts on clear shrink plastic. *Note: Lightly sand shrink plastic before stamping hearts.* Cut out hearts; punch 1⁄16-inch holes at top of each and shrink with heat tool. Attach hearts to tag by threading silver wire through hearts and threading the wire back through hole in tag. Twist and curl wire to secure.

Use a computer or hand-print "Be My Valentine" onto white card stock; cut a 2¼ x 7¼-inch rectangle around words with decorative-edge scissors. Center and adhere to bag. Randomly stamp hearts onto tissue paper and insert paper into bag.

Attach embellished tag to top of bag with adhesive foam squares; tie heart-print ribbon around handle. ∎

SOURCES: Rubber stamps and red dye ink pad from Stampin' Up!; solvent-based ink pad from Tsukineko.

MATERIALS

- Small red gift bag
- White card stock
- White tissue paper
- 2-inch round metal-edge tag
- White shrink plastic
- Valentine sentiment and heart rubber stamps
- Red solvent-based ink pad
- Red dye ink pad
- ¼- and 1⁄16-inch hole punches
- Heart-print ribbon
- Double-sided adhesive sheets
- Clear micro beads
- 30-gauge silver wire
- Decorative-edge scissors
- ¼-inch adhesive foam squares
- Fine sandpaper
- Heat tool
- Computer font (optional)

⊣ WRAPS ⊢

Wrapped Soaps

Designs by MARY LYNN MALONEY

MATERIALS
- Bars of soap
- 7 x 10-inch patterned scrapbook papers
- Clock face rubber stamp
- Swirled line rubber stamp
- Brown, dark blue and light blue ink pads
- Purple and light blue craft wire
- Assorted glass beads
- Jewelry pliers
- Double-sided tape

Use printed sheets of scrapbook paper to create easy and interesting wraps for luxurious bath soaps.

Randomly stamp clock face image onto patterned paper with brown ink; repeat process with swirled line rubber stamp and dark blue or light blue ink. Let inks dry. Wrap soap with stamped paper. Wrap purple or light blue wire randomly around wrapped soap, threading beads as desired. Secure beads by curling wire around end of jewelry pliers. Twist wire ends together on bottom of soap to secure. ■

SOURCES: Patterned paper from K&Company; rubber stamps from Renaissance Art Stamps and Magenta; Fun Wire from Toner Plastics.

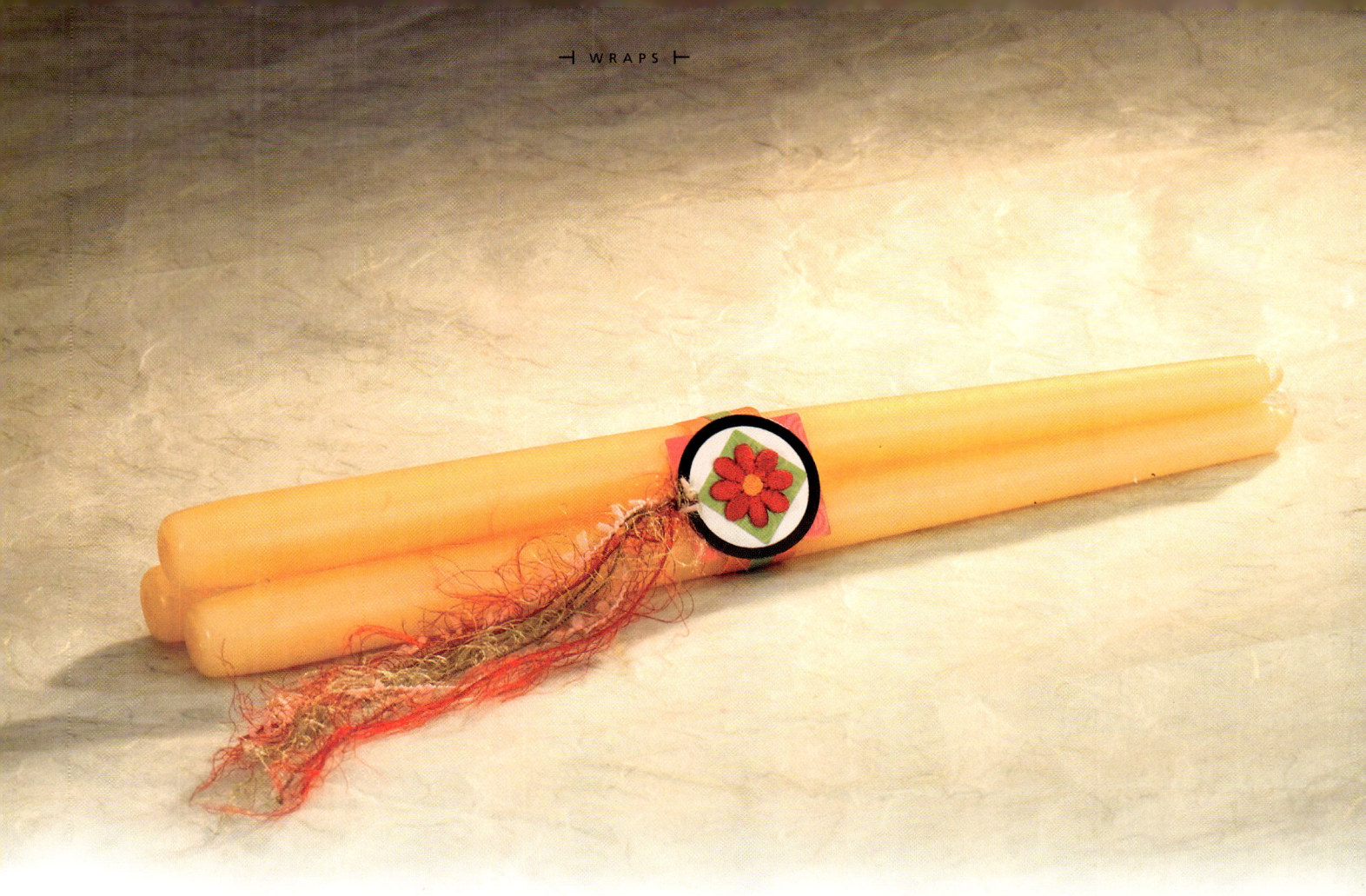

Colorful Candle Band

Design by MARY LYNN MALONEY

Make a simple gift of classic taper candles really special with a colorful band that has lots of textural appeal.

Center and adhere green square sticker to circle tag; attach flower appliqué to green square with fabric adhesive. Cut 12-inch lengths of assorted fibers; loop fibers through hole in tag.

Cut a 7-inch-long strip of an orange sticker and lay onto parchment paper. Cut a 7-inch-long strip of a narrow green sticker; center and adhere to orange sticker strip. Use gem adhesive to attach circle tag to a pink rectangle sticker; center and adhere assembled piece onto layered sticker strip. Wrap strip around taper candles securing papers in the back with a small push pin. ■

SOURCES: Stickers from EK Success; circle tag from DMD Inc.; Fabri-Tac and Gem-Tac adhesives from Beacon.

MATERIALS
3 (12-inch) ivory taper candles
Black-edged circle tag
Pink, green and orange assorted shape stickers
Pink flower appliqué
Pink and green fibers
Small push pin
Small square parchment baking paper
Fabric adhesive
Gem adhesive

Baby Thank-You Set

Design by JACQUELINE JONES

A new mom-to-be would love to receive this handmade set of thank-you cards, just in time to send thanks for baby gifts! DIAGRAM ON PAGE 83

MATERIALS
- White card stock
- Light purple mulberry paper
- Envelopes
- Diaper pin and "Thank you for the baby gift" rubber stamps
- Black ink pad
- Clear embossing powder
- Watercolor pencils
- Water brush pen
- Sheer purple ribbon
- Adhesive foam dots
- Embossing heat tool
- Decorative-edge scissors
- Craft knife

Cut several 5½ x 8½-inch pieces of white card stock; score and fold each in half. Stamp and emboss "Thank you" image onto the front of each card toward the bottom; stamp and emboss two diaper pin images above "Thank you." Use watercolor pencils and water brush pen to color the top of each diaper pin.

Stamp and emboss one diaper pin image for each card onto a separate sheet of white card stock; color in same manner as above. Cut out images and attach one to each card with adhesive foam dots.

To make portfolio, cut a 9⅛ x 14¼-inch piece of white card stock. Referring to diagram, measure and cut out portfolio; score and fold dashed lines. Turn portfolio over and stamp outside surface randomly with diaper pin image. Use watercolors and water brush pen to apply color to diaper pins. Cut top edge of portfolio with decorative-edge scissors; cut a piece of light purple mulberry paper to fit inside portfolio. Adhere mulberry paper inside; allow a small amount to peek out at top.

With a craft knife, cut a small slit toward top of portfolio as indicated on diagram. Fold portfolio up and mark placement of two additional slits in bottom portion; cut slits. **Note:** *The top slit in the bottom portion must meet up with the first slit when portfolio is folded.* Assemble portfolio and insert ribbon through slits to tie shut. ∎

SOURCES: Rubber stamps from Biblical Impressions and Denami Design.

Chick Flick DVD Wrap

Design by ANNIE LANG

Skip the wrapping paper and tuck a DVD in this adorable sleeve for your next gift-giving occasion.

Use sponge-tip applicator to apply orange chalk to each bird's beak, feet, cheeks and along edges. With fine-tip black marker, add a loose outline and detail lines to both die-cuts. Attach purple fibers around each bird's head; secure ends in front with satin bow embellishment and an adhesive dot.

Adhere each bird to black card stock; cut around bird leaving a narrow border. Leave a thicker border around bird's feet for added support. Cut along the bottom perforated lines beneath the beak of one bird.

Position die-cuts with back sides together; insert DVD case between them to determine placement of adhesive. Adhere chosen areas to create the DVD sleeve.

Layer a 3½ x 4½-inch white paper rectangle onto a 4 x 5-inch black card stock rectangle. Cut a 4 x 5-inch rectangle from blue patterned paper and adhere to back side of black card stock. Add a personalized message to white side; tri-fold card so side edges meet in the center. Attach small eyelets to the center edges of the folded card. Thread twine through eyelets and tie into a bow. Tuck card into bird's beak.

SOURCES: Die-cuts from AccuCut.

MATERIALS
DVD case
2 large bird-with-face yellow card stock die-cuts
Black card stock
Blue patterned paper
White paper
Orange chalk
Sponge-tip applicator
Black fine-tip marker
2 small blue eyelets
6 inches twine
2 (4-inch) purple fibers
2 small pink ribbon bow embellishments
Adhesive dots

Dream Stars

Designs by ANNIE LANG

MATERIALS

- Several 12 x 12-inch sheets bright decorative paper
- 2 (12 x 12-inch) sheets black card stock
- 2 (12 x 12-inch) sheets white card stock
- 1 (12 x 12-inch) sheet bright yellow card stock
- Standard-size pencil box
- Heavy-duty hook-and-loop tab
- 1½ x 6½-inch strip white poster board
- ¾-inch jewel-toned flat-back heart
- 16 inches decorative trim cord
- 4 (2½-inch) lengths pink metallic embroidery floss
- Small round translucent pink scrapbook nails
- Blue and clear glitter glue
- Acid-free white glue
- Glass and bead glue
- Watercolor markers
- Colored pencils
- Chalks
- Black and gray fine-tip markers
- Ruler
- Hole starter tool

Pick photos with sentimental meaning and create this fun-to-make set that's a gift and wrap all in one!

DIAGRAMS ON PAGE 83–85

Greeting Card

Enlarge star pocket pattern 120 percent and transfer it onto white card stock; color stars as desired. Outline and add detail lines with black fine-tip marker. Cut out image and adhere to black card stock; cut around image leaving a narrow border.

Referring to photo, measure and fold card "accordion-style" into three sections. Apply a line of acid-free white glue along the top left edge of card to create a pocket.

Use patterns to transfer inside and outside card verses onto white card stock. Cut out and outline both with black marker. Transfer four of the desired star patterns to white card stock; color in images. Outline and add detail lines. Cut out stars. Adhere one star to lower right corner of outside verse and tuck into card pocket. Adhere remaining rectangle inside card; apply clear glitter glue around edges and attach remaining stars next to message.

Gift Box

Project note: *Any size box may be used. Piece and glue decorative paper sections together to fit the size box that is being covered. Use box diagram as a guide.*

With pattern side of decorative paper face down, measure 2¼ inches up from bottom edge; mark as a starting line with a pencil. Place box onto marked line; trace outline of box. This will be the baseline measuring guide; refer to the box diagram to calculate measuring lines for remaining box areas. For each tab on diagram, allow at least ¼ inch to be folded over box edges. Once measuring is finished, cut out paper sections and adhere sections to box. Cut a piece of paper to fit inside lid; adhere.

Attach one side of the hook-and-loop tab to the center of the box lid approximately 1½ inches from edge. Cover poster board strip with decorative paper; attach remaining side of hook-and-loop tab to strip. Attach the closure strip to the box lid; fold strip over edge and around to box bottom. Glue strip sections firmly in place.

Referring to photo, transfer only the bottom portion of the star pocket pattern to white card stock; color in image. Adhere to black card stock and trim leaving a narrow border. Apply a line of acid-free glue along the bottom and left edges of star motif; attach to box lid edge to create a pocket. Use glass and bead glue to adhere jewel-toned heart to the front closure tab.

Stand box upright; measure 2 inches down on both side edges and use hole starter tool to begin a hole on each side. Thread decorative cord ends through holes; tie a knot at each end inside box to form handle. Apply turquoise glitter to each of the stars' noses and along closure tab edge.

continued on page 47

⊣ WRAPS ⊢

Graduation Memories

Design by DONNA CHAPMAN FOR DMD, INC.

MATERIALS

- 12 x 12-inch sheets purple, turquoise, gold, orange and brown card stock
- 5 x 7-inch brown mini file folder
- 4 light blue eyelets
- 1-inch letter stencils
- ½-inch alphabet rubber stamps
- Small alphabet rubber stamps
- Polka-dotted circle rubber stamp
- Black and brown ink pads
- Duster brush
- Craft knife
- Ruler
- Glue stick
- Adhesive foam dots
- Photocopier
- CD case

Personalize the liner of a CD case by reducing and copying a special scrapbook page!

Cut a 1 x 12-inch strip of purple card stock; cut a strip of orange card stock the same size. Use black ink to stamp polka-dotted circle stamp on both strips; overlap each circle slightly. Cut a ½ x 12-inch strip of gold card stock; stamp ½-inch ABCs across strip. Stamp ABCs across the top edge of a 5½ x 12-inch strip of gold card stock; cut a 4 x 12-inch strip from turquoise card stock.

For pocket, cut a 5½ x 12-inch strip of orange card stock; fold in half to create a 2¾ x 12-inch pocket. Punch a hole in each pocket corner; secure pocket by attaching eyelets in each hole. Glue stamped orange strip to pocket.

Glue the stamped purple strip toward the top of a 12 x 12-inch sheet of purple card stock; adhere gold strip slightly down from stamped strip; glue turquoise strip slightly down from gold strip. Glue assembled pocket on top of turquoise strip. Attach photo to left side of page with adhesive foam dots.

Trace desired letter stencils onto brown card stock; cut them out. **Note:** *Use smaller stencils if using a longer name. Stamp a few letters with polka-dotted circle stamp; add brown ink to other letters using a duster brush. Position letters onto page; adhere some with glue stick and others with adhesive foam dots.*

For journal file, glue a couple of colored card stock strips across front of file folder and trim edges even. Stamp date and grade onto strips with small alphabet stamps. Write journaling onto a piece of card stock and tuck it into file folder; place folder into pocket.

For CD case, reduce the 12 x 12-inch scrapbook page by 45 percent on a photocopier. Trim the edges to fit and slide into a CD case. Stamp ABCs onto card stock with brown ink; cut to fit into the left edge area of CD case and insert. ∎

SOURCES: Card stock and mini file folder from DMD Inc.; letter stencils from Duro Art; small alphabet rubber stamps from Hero Arts.

Annie's Attic, Berne, IN 46711 • AnniesAttic.com • All Wrapped Up | 45

⊣ WRAPS ⊢

Spooky Paint Cans
Designs by MARY AYRES

MATERIALS
- 2-quart paint cans
- Card stock: orange, black, yellow, purple, white and green
- Old newspaper patterned paper and golden brown striped paper
- Gray and black fibers
- Narrow sisal cord
- 10 (⅛-inch) round silver eyelets
- Spiderweb rubber stamp
- Black ink pad
- Craft sponge
- Decorative-edge scissors
- Instant-dry paper adhesive
- 1¼-, 1/16- and ⅛-inch circle punches
- Computer font (optional)

Embellish everyday paint cans with paper and fill them with Halloween candy or popcorn for cute gift items.

DIAGRAM ON PAGE 86

For ghost can, cut newspaper patterned paper to fit around paint can and adhere. With decorative-edge scissors, cut a 3¼-inch diameter circle from purple card stock. Apply black ink to edges with craft sponge. Use pattern provided to cut out a ghost from white card stock with decorative-edge scissors. Apply black ink to edges and glue ghost to purple circle.

Stamp spiderwebs onto circle around ghost. Punch two ⅛-inch holes as indicated on pattern for eyes; attach eyelets. Referring to photo, punch 1/16-inch holes beside ghost as indicated on pattern and insert gray fiber in and out through holes. Glue ends in back.

Punch a ⅛-inch hole on both sides of purple circle near edge; attach eyelets. Insert sisal cord through both eyelets starting with the left; wrap around paint can. Tie cording in a knot at left eyelet; trim ends and unravel.

Cut a 3⅛-inch diameter circle from orange card stock with decorative-edge scissors. Apply black ink to edges. Stamp spiderwebs onto circle and adhere to top of paint can lid.

For tag, use a computer or hand-print "Boo to you!" onto green card stock. Cut a rectangle around words with decorative-edge scissors. Stamp spiderwebs onto tag and apply black ink to edges. Punch a ⅛-inch hole at side of tag and attach an eyelet. Wrap sisal cord around bottom of can and tie into a knot at top; thread sisal cord end through tag and knot ends together.

For spider can, follow same basic instructions as above but use golden brown striped paper instead of newspaper patterned paper, yellow card stock instead of green and reverse the orange and purple circles.

To make spider, punch a 1¼-inch circle from black card stock for body and glue onto orange circle. Punch two ⅛-inch holes toward top of body for eyes; attach eyelets. Punch eight 1/16-inch holes on body referring to photo for placement; punch eight additional 1/16-inch holes stemming out from body holes. Insert black fibers through holes creating spider legs; secure ends in back with glue.

SOURCES: Patterned paper from K&Company; PSX rubber stamp from Duncan; Zip Dry paper adhesive from Beacon.

Dream Stars DIAGRAMS ON PAGE 83–85
continued from page 42

Scrapbook Pages

For large photo page, mount photo onto yellow card stock; trim edges to ¼ inch. Use patterns to transfer star pocket, a small star and one of the cloud verses to white card stock; color images and cut out. Layer each onto black card stock; trim leaving a narrow border. Apply a line of glue along left and bottom edges of star pocket; attach to left side of a 12 x 12-inch sheet of decorative paper. Insert photo partially into pocket; secure photo with glue if desired. Adhere cloud verse and star to lower right corner of photo.

For remaining page, cut yellow card stock into diamond shapes; adhere diamond shapes behind photos. Arrange and adhere photos to a 12 x 12-inch sheet of decorative paper. Outline edges with black and gray markers.

Transfer remaining cloud verse and a few small and medium stars onto white card stock; color images and cut out. Outline edges with black marker. Adhere cloud and two stars in lower left corner of page.

Create holes in photo corners; insert pink scrapbook nails. Adhere remaining stars above photos. If desired, glue metallic embroidery floss from top nails to stars to form photo hangers.

SOURCES: Aleene's Memory Glue and Aleene's Platinum Bond Glass and Bead Slick Surface Adhesive from Duncan.

Fruit Gift Set

Designs by JACQUELINE JONES

MATERIALS

- 12 x 12-inch sheets ivory mulberry paper
- Ivory, light brown and brown card stock
- Peach mulberry paper
- Watercolor paper
- Takeout box template
- Pale gold, gray and black ink pads
- Assorted fruit and sentiment rubber stamps
- Clear embossing powder
- Opalescent transparent paints
- Sheer ribbon
- Assorted fibers
- Gold eyelets
- Purple eyelet
- 2 brown buttons
- Ultra-fine glitter
- Clear-drying adhesive
- Double-sided tape
- Adhesive foam squares
- Heat embossing tool
- Paintbrush
- Paper trimmer with scoring tool
- Hook-and-loop closures
- Hole punch

Enclose fruit and nuts in these tiny stamped boxes and wraps, and add to a wicker basket for a quick and easy elegant gift. DIAGRAM ON PAGE 86

Fruit Wraps

Randomly stamp assorted fruit images onto ivory mulberry paper with pale gold ink; let dry. Stamp desired sentiment onto light brown card stock; cut a rounded tag shape around sentiment. Tear side edge and punch a hole in tag. Wrap stamped mulberry paper around fruit. Thread tag onto sheer ribbon or fibers and tie around stamped paper to close.

Card

Cut a 6½ x 10-inch piece of ivory card stock; score and fold in half. Use gray ink to stamp assorted fruit images onto card. Use black ink and clear embossing powder to stamp and emboss assorted fruit images onto a 4⅝ x 3½-inch piece of ivory card stock; color images with opalescent transparent paint. Apply clear-drying adhesive to fruit and sprinkle on ultra-fine glitter; shake off excess and let dry.

Trim top edge of fruit so that the border follows the fruit outlines. Mat motif onto a 4⅞ x 3-inch brown rectangle; mat again onto a 4⅞ x 3¼-inch light brown rectangle. Mount onto card front.

Cut a 1½ x 3-inch rectangle from light brown card stock; round top two corners to form a tag shape. Punch a hole at top of tag; attach an eyelet and loop several fibers through eyelet. Stamp desired sentiment onto ivory card stock; cut a 1¼-inch square around sentiment and mount onto a 1½-inch dark brown square. Attach layered square to tag and attach tag to card with adhesive foam squares.

Takeout Boxes

Use takeout box template to trace and cut out desired number of boxes. Assemble boxes using double-sided tape. Stamp and emboss fruit images onto watercolor paper; add color with opalescent transparent paints and let dry. Cut out images. Tear small pieces of peach mulberry paper; adhere one piece to the front and back of each box. Adhere a colored fruit image on top of mulberry paper pieces.

Punch a hole on each side of boxes; attach eyelets. Thread fibers through eyelets; tie knots inside box to secure handle.

Button Box

Enlarge button box pattern 123 percent; use pattern to trace and cut out button box from light brown card stock. Cut on solid lines; score and fold on dashed lines. Assemble with double-sided tape. Attach hook-and-loop closure under flap; attach buttons with adhesive squares. ■

SOURCES: Rubber stamps from Biblical Impressions and Anna Griffin; box template from The C-Thru Ruler Co.; Radiant Pearls transparent paint from LuminArte.

Halloween Fun CD Pocket

Design by ANNIE LANG

MATERIALS

Die-cuts: large white ghost, orange pumpkin, large white bat and two small white bats
Black card stock
Chalks
Sponge-tip applicators
Black fine- and medium-tip markers
White gel pen
Adhesive dots
¼-inch double-sided tape
Ruler

Keep track of Halloween memories with a photo CD presented in this whimsical card.

Use sponge-tip applicator to apply blue chalk to edges and along perforated lines on ghost die-cut. Apply red chalk to nose and cheeks. Repeat for the pumpkin using red chalk for nose and cheeks and green chalk for stem. Color large bat with bright green chalk; color small bats with bright orange and purple chalk. Add open mouth areas with medium-tip marker; add loose outline and detail lines with fine-tip marker.

Score and fold one 8½ x 11-inch sheet of black card stock in half; unfold card and place face up on work surface. Adhere ghost die-cut to card front and fold overlapping left edge to back of card. Trim bottom of ghost even with card. Attach purple bat to back of card with adhesive dots.

Flip card over to inside; adhere large bat die-cut inside center of card. Attach remaining bat in lower left corner.

Cut a 6-inch square from black card stock; measure and mark a ¼-inch border around three sides of the square. Score and fold along these lines to create pocket tabs. Clip the bottom tab corners so pocket will lie flat. Attach pumpkin to front of pocket; trim along top edge of pocket to follow pumpkin stem shape. Apply ¼-inch-wide double-sided tape to pocket tabs and adhere along bottom inside edge.

Use gel pen to write a personalized message on the front and inside of card. Add stitch marks along pocket edges and swirl lines around bats. ■

SOURCES: Die-cuts from AccuCut.

Itty Bitty Surprise Card

Design by LAURIE D'AMBROSIO

Delight your holiday sweetheart with a tiny piece of jewelry or other treasure tucked inside the mini keepsake bag.

MATERIALS
- White textured card stock
- Red sparkle card stock
- Green hologram paper
- White matte-finish embossing paper
- Red mini keepsake bag
- Silver glitter embossing powder
- 2½-inch square template
- Heat tool
- Craft knife
- ⅛-inch round anywhere punch
- Wooden mallet
- Self-healing cutting mat
- Adhesive dots
- Computer font (optional)

Cut white textured card stock to 5¼ x 8½ inches; score and fold in half. On front of card, measure and cut a 2-inch square opening. Cut a 3½-inch square from green hologram paper; adhere inside card with paper showing through opening. Use the craft knife to cut a 2-inch square from red sparkle card stock; discard square. Use the 2½-inch template to cut a frame around the red sparkle square opening; adhere red sparkle frame around the 2-inch square opening.

Use a computer to print "Merry Christmas" in desired font and color onto embossing paper; sprinkle with embossing powder and emboss with heat tool. ***Note:*** *Desired message can also be stamped or hand-printed with embossing ink instead of using a computer.* Cut out message; mount onto red sparkle card stock. Trim card stock leaving a small border; adhere to card below opening.

Lay card on cutting mat; place a small gift into mini bag and pull closed. Position bag on top of hologram paper showing through opening. Use anywhere punch and wooden mallet to punch a hole on each side of bag. Wrap ribbon around bag and thread through holes tying ribbon on back of card. ■

SOURCES: Keepsake bag from Blumenthal Lansing Co.; embossing paper and embossing powder from Creative Beginnings; hologram paper from New Dimensions; red sparkle card stock from Making Memories.

Winter Memories

Design by ANNIE LANG

MATERIALS
Die-cuts: 2 large snowflakes and one small snowflake with faces
2 (8½ x 11-inch) sheets light blue card stock
Very fine iridescent glitter
Light blue and pink chalk
Black fine-tip marker
Craft sponge
Sponge-tip applicator
Ruler
Adhesive dots
¼-inch-wide double-sided tape

Make your winter memories extra special by presenting them in this fun keepsake greeting card, complete with a pocket sized to fit a CD.

Apply light blue chalk along edges and along perforated lines of each snowflake with sponge-tip applicator. Add pink chalk to the cheek and nose areas. Use black fine-tip marker to create a loose outline around each snowflake; add detail lines along perforated lines and facial details.

Score and fold one light blue card stock sheet in half; unfold card and lay face up on work surface. Adhere one of the large snowflakes to card front; fold left edges of snowflake around to back of card and trim right edge. Adhere remaining large snowflake inside; trim all edges even with card.

Cut a 6-inch square from light blue card stock; measure and mark a ¼-inch border along three sides of the square. Score and fold along these lines to create pocket tabs. Clip the bottom tab corners so pocket will lie flat. Adhere small snowflake to front of pocket; trim along top of pocket to follow snowflake's shape. Apply double-sided tape to each pocket tab. Line up pocket and adhere along inside edges. ***Note:*** *Pocket will overlap large snowflake.* Use a craft sponge to apply a light layer of very fine iridescent glitter to desired areas. Use black marker to add a personalized message on inside and outside of card; insert a CD into pocket. ■

SOURCE: Die-cuts from AccuCut.

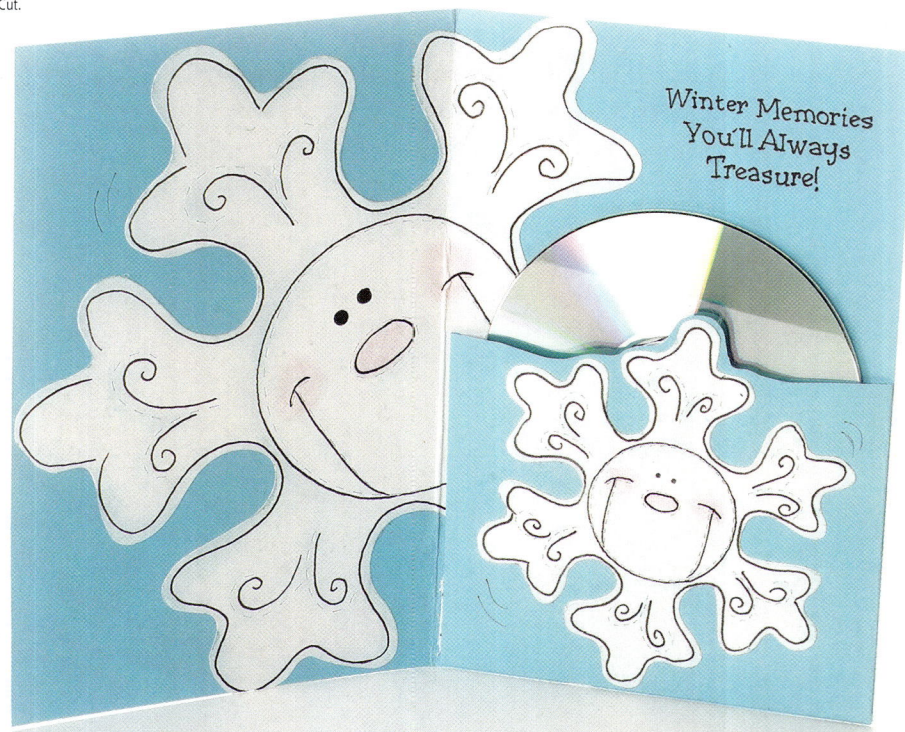

WRAPS

Vellum Heart Totes

Design by MARGARET HANSON-MADDOX

Candy treats are right at home in these tiny totes with vellum accents. DIAGRAM ON PAGE 87

Referring to diagram, score and fold dashed lines on double-sided yellow/purple card stock with purple side face down. Punch heart border design along top edge; adhere yellow patterned paper to the purple side. Fold tote up to determine placement of heart; unfold and cut out heart using heart template and craft knife. Glue vellum square to the back side of cutout heart. Fold totes up and punch two holes at top of tote through all layers. Fill plastic bag with candy and staple inside tote. Thread light purple ribbon through holes and tie into a bow.

For mint green tote, follow basic instructions above, but use mint green card stock instead of double-sided card stock, rose print vellum instead of white vellum, flower border punch instead of heart border punch and white voile ribbon instead of light purple ribbon. Do not cut out heart for mint green tote. ■

SOURCES: Card stock, rose print vellum, border punches and heart template from Fiskars; yellow patterned paper from Hot Off The Press.

MATERIALS

- 4½ x 10½-inch double-sided yellow/purple card stock
- 4½ x 10½-inch mint green card stock
- 3⅞ x 9¹³⁄₁₆-inch yellow patterned paper
- 4 x 10-inch rose print vellum
- 2-inch square white vellum
- 16 inches light purple ribbon
- 16 inches white wire-edge voile ribbon
- 5½ x 9-inch clear plastic bags
- Heart border and flower border punches
- Heart template
- ¼-inch circle punch
- Craft knife
- Paper trimmer
- Scorer
- Stapler with staples
- Ruler
- Glue stick
- Candy

Winter Gift Pail

Design by MARY AYRES

MATERIALS
- 2-quart metal pail
- White card stock
- White vellum
- Glittery patterned vellum
- Light purple striped paper
- Assorted embossed and flat stickers
- Blue tag sticker
- Vintage buttons
- 3 (3/16-inch) silver eyelets
- 4 small silver brads
- Silver heart charm
- 1/2-inch-wide sheer wired silver ribbon
- 1/8-inch-wide wired silver ribbon
- 1/8-inch-wide blue silk ribbon
- Ultra-fine iridescent glitter
- Blue ink pad
- 1/16- and 3/16-inch circle punches
- Sewing machine with silver sewing thread
- Small craft sponges
- Computer font (optional)
- Instant-dry paper adhesive
- Gem adhesive

Give your holiday gifts in style by packaging them in a simple metal pail dressed up with pretty embellishments such as vellum, charms and ribbon.

Cut a 4½ x 6-inch rectangle from white card stock; attach stickers in lower right and upper left corners. Tear two rectangles from two chosen areas of glittery patterned vellum; adhere in upper right and lower left corners. Use a zigzag stitch to machine-sew around inside edges of vellum rectangles.

Tear a 5 x 6½-inch rectangle from light purple striped paper; add iridescent glitter to edges. Glue card stock rectangle onto striped paper; machine-stitch around rectangle and apply blue ink to edges.

Adhere blue tag sticker to vellum; tear vellum around tag and apply blue ink to edges. Punch a 3/16-inch hole at top of tag. Cut a 6-inch piece of 1/8-inch-wide wired silver ribbon; insert ribbon ends through tag. Bring ends back through formed loop and pull taut. Trim ribbon ends and glue tag across card stock rectangle. Attach stickers in open areas.

Use a computer or hand-print "hope … joy … peace" onto vellum; tear a 1¼ x 3½-inch rectangle around words and apply blue ink to edges. Add glitter to edges and attach rectangle to tag by inserting a brad in each corner. Thread blue ribbon through silver heart charm and tie into a bow; trim ends and glue heart to tag.

Adhere buttons to desired areas of card stock. Punch two 3/16-inch holes on each side of tag; attach eyelets. Beginning from back, insert both ends of a piece of 1/2-inch-wide wired silver ribbon through eyelets. Glue rectangle to pail. Wrap another piece of 1/2-inch-wide wired silver ribbon around pail; connect ends with ribbon ends sticking through eyelets and tie into bows. Trim ends even.

For tag, use a computer or hand-print "celebrate" onto white card stock. Cut a 1 x 4¼-inch rectangle around word and apply blue ink to edges. Adhere word rectangle to a 1¾ x 5-inch piece of vellum; tear edges of vellum and apply blue ink and glitter to edges. Use a zigzag stitch to machine-sew around word rectangle.

Adhere a button onto two layered button stickers; attach to left side of tag. Punch a 3/16-inch hole in tag; attach an eyelet. Insert both ends of a 6-inch piece of 1/2-inch-wide sheer wired ribbon through eyelet; pull ends back through formed loop and pull taut. Trim ends and tie tag to handle. ■

SOURCES: Glittered vellum, striped paper, tag and embossed stickers from K&Company; stickers from EK Success; Zip Dry and Gem-Tac adhesives from Beacon.

Valentine's Day Party Cones

Designs by LORETTA MATEIK

MATERIALS
Red patterned paper
White vellum
Red and white card stock
White tissue paper
Heart and "love"
　rubber stamps
Red ink pad
Red marker
3 white buttons
¼- and ¹⁄₁₆-inch
　hole punches
1 brass square brad
1 red square brad
White and red
　satin cording
Adhesive foam dots
Paper crimper

Decorate for Valentine's Day with pretty paper cones filled with dried flowers or candies. DIAGRAMS ON PAGE 87–88

Enlarge triangle pattern 110 percent; trace pattern onto white card stock and cut out. Use large heart pattern to cut one heart from red card stock; run through paper crimper. Apply lines to white triangle with red marker to add a plaid pattern. Roll triangle into a cone shape; fold down overlapping ends in back. Punch a ¹⁄₁₆-inch hole through folded down layers and use red square brad to secure.

Punch a ¼-inch hole on each side of cone; thread red cording through holes and tie a knot on each side to form a handle.

Glue buttons to heart; secure heart to front of cone with adhesive foam dots. Randomly stamp hearts onto white tissue paper; cut a 7-inch square from stamped tissue and tuck into cone.

To create red cone, use red patterned paper instead of white card stock, white cording instead of red and use small heart pattern to cut a small heart from vellum. Stamp with "love" image and attach to cone in same manner as above. ■

SOURCES: Patterned paper from Making Memories; rubber stamps, ink pad and marker from Stampin' Up!.

⊣ BOXES ⊢

Glass Petal Tins

Design by MARY AYRES

Create tiny embellished tins for your favorite season! Small and simple, these tins hold handmade candies or other little treasures.

Lightly sand tin and paint white; let dry. Cut a rectangle from blue patterned paper that measures the same size as top of tin lid. Trim corners with rounded corner edger. Apply blue ink to edges of rectangle and glue to lid.

Cut a 2 x 2¾-inch rectangle from white card stock; cut top two corners diagonally to form a tag shape. Use a zigzag stitch to machine-sew around tag with green thread. Punch a 3/16-inch hole at top of tag and attach eyelet. Insert both ends of a piece of ribbon through eyelet; bring ends back through loop and pull taut. Trim ends in V-notches; glue tag to lid.

Use a computer or hand-print "happy easter" onto white card stock. Spray words with spray fixative and place clear blue stone on top of words; cut around edge. Brush a thick layer of gem adhesive on back of stone and adhere to word circle. Wipe sandpaper across paper edge to sand it even with stone.

Punch seven flower petals from pink card stock; apply pink ink to edges. Glue petals under blue stone and bend petals upward. Stamp ivy leaf image onto green card stock using green ink; cut out leaf. Score and fold along vein lines; glue leaf and flower to tag.

To make "spring blossom" tin, follow same instructions as above but use golden yellow patterned paper instead of blue paper, orange stone instead of blue stone and orange ink instead of pink and blue ink. ■

SOURCES: Patterned papers from Hot Off The Press and K&Company; glass picture pebbles from JudiKins; rubber stamp from Delta/Rubber Stampede; petal punch from Emagination Crafts; workable fixative from Krylon; Zip Dry and Gem-Tac adhesives from Beacon.

MATERIALS
2 metal tins
Card stock: white, yellow, green and pink
Golden yellow and blue patterned papers
White acrylic paint
Blue and orange clear glass stones
2 (3/16-inch) round silver eyelets
2 (6-inch-long) pieces ⅝-inch-wide green ribbon
Ivy leaf rubber stamp
Ink pads: green, blue, orange and pink
Rounded corner edger
Flower petal punch
3/16-inch circle punch
Sewing machine with green sewing thread
Craft sponge
Paintbrush
Spray fixative
Instant-dry paper adhesive
Gem adhesive
Rotary tool and scoring blade
Sandpaper
Computer font (optional)

Folded Floral Gift Set

Designs by LORINE MASON

MATERIALS
- 2 (12 x 12-inch) sheets floral print paper
- 2 (12 x 12-inch) sheets pink paper
- White card stock
- White paper
- Flower petal punch
- 1/16- and 1/4-inch hole punches
- 1/2 yd 1/4-inch-wide pink satin ribbon
- 2 yards 1-inch-wide pink satin ribbon
- Clear micro beads
- Pink pearl bead
- Stylus
- Decorative-edge scissors
- Clothespins
- Ruler
- Paper trimmer
- Instant-dry paper adhesive
- Glue stick

Pretty ribbon and beads add to the elegant feminine look of this set. Use decorative-edge scissors for quick embellishment. DIAGRAMS ON PAGE 88

Gift Box

Cut four 8-inch diameter circles from floral print paper; cut four 8-inch diameter circles from pink paper. Cut one 8-inch diameter circle from white paper. Use glue stick to adhere the floral-print and pink circles together; cut edges with decorative-edge scissors. Punch tiny holes around perimeter of each circle with the 1/16-inch hole punch.

Fold the 8-inch diameter white paper circle in half; fold the half into thirds forming a cone shape. Unfold the circle. Referring to diagram, mark three equal points of an equilateral triangle from the six fold divisions. *Note: The dashed lines on the diagram represent the fold lines; the solid lines show the placement of the marks.* This circle will now act as a pattern. Use pattern to mark the three points on each of the printed circles cut previously; connect the three points on the printed circles with a ruler and stylus to create a triangle in the center of each. *Note: Draw triangle on solid pink side.*

On three of the circles, fold two sides of the triangle outwards; fold remaining side inwards. Fold all sides of the remaining circle inward and lay it flat on work surface; apply glue to each folded flap on this circle. Place one circle at a time on top of bottom circle and adhere the bottom inward-folded flap; repeat for remaining circles and use clothespins to hold circles in place until completely dry. Remove clothespins and use the 1/4-inch hole punch to punch holes at the top of each section. Thread 1-inch-wide ribbon through holes; tie a bow.

Card

Cut a 4 x 8 1/4-inch rectangle from white card stock; score and fold in half. Cut a 2 x 8 1/4-inch strip from floral-print paper; cut one long edge with decorative-edge scissors. Punch holes along edge with 1/16-inch hole punch. Adhere to bottom edge of card with decorative edge facing upward. Cut bottom edge of card with decorative-edge scissors and add holes along edge with 1/16-inch hole punch.

Cut a strip of 1/4-inch-wide ribbon; adhere in center of floral-print strip on card and trim ends. Punch out several flower petals; add dimension to petals by carefully folding them in half slightly. Begin to layer petals on top of each other creating a flower; glue micro beads and pink pearl in center of flower. Fold a 4-inch piece of 1/4-inch-wide satin ribbon in half. Cut a small slit in seam of card; insert ribbon ends through slit and glue ends inside card. ■

SOURCES: Flower petal punch from Emagination Crafts; Zip Dry paper adhesive from Beacon.

⊣ BOXES ⊢

Annie's Attic, Berne, IN 46711 • AnniesAttic.com • All Wrapped Up | 59

Baby Carriage Gift Box

Design by SANDY ROLLINGER

MATERIALS
- 4 x 6-inch box
- Pink patterned paper
- Dark pink and pink papers
- White card stock
- White and pink paper paints
- 2-inch circle punch
- 1-inch flower punch
- ½-inch flower punch
- 1-inch-wide gathered white lace trim
- ¼-inch-wide pink satin ribbon
- White chenille stem
- Double-sided adhesive sheets
- Nonstick scissors
- Paper trimmer
- Instant-dry paper adhesive
- Cellophane tape
- Scrap paper

Shaped like a baby buggy, this is one package the mom-to-be is sure to keep! Tiny baby gifts will fit easily in the compact box.

Place desired gift in box; wrap box with pink patterned paper. Cut a 1½-inch-wide strip of dark pink paper long enough to fit around the center of the box plus ½ inch. Attach strip to adhesive sheet; trim sheet to fit strip and adhere to box. Make dots on strip with white paper paint; let dry.

Use the 2-inch circle punch to make four circles from white card stock; attach each circle to adhesive sheets. Attach pink paper to other side of adhesive sheets; use nonstick scissors to cut excess adhesive and paper around card stock circles. Punch out four flowers from white card stock using large flower punch; use smaller flower punch to punch out four flowers from pink paper. Use paper adhesive to adhere a pink flower to white flower; repeat for remaining flowers and apply a dot of white paper paint to each flower's center. Glue a flower to each pink circle and add dots to circles with white paper paint.

Cut a 5 x 8-inch rectangle from white card stock; adhere dark pink paper to white card stock with adhesive sheet. Cut a piece of scrap paper the same size; fold scrap paper in half and round off corners to make an oval pattern. Place pattern on dark pink rectangle and cut out oval with nonstick scissors. Use flower punches to punch out two large white flowers and two small pink flowers; layer a pink flower on top of a white flower. Repeat for remaining two flowers and add a dot of white paper paint to each flower's center; let dry. Adhere a flower toward each end of oval.

Attach lace trim around the edge of the oval and around the bottom edge of the dark pink band around box. Glue pink satin ribbon to edges of paper band. Referring to photo, fold white chenille stem into thirds to form a handle; curl ends and glue into place. Attach pink circles to bottom of box to act as wheels. Referring to photo, fold dark pink oval over end of box to form the "bonnet." Apply glue under each rounded end; hold in place until dry. Add a small pink bow to bonnet. ■

SOURCES: Paper paints from Plaid; PeelnStick double-sided adhesive sheets from Therm O Web; Zip Dry paper adhesive from Beacon.

⊣ BOXES ⊢

Paper Marigold Box

Design by SANDY ROLLINGER

Give a gift nestled inside a box embellished with the cheery touch of fringed paper flowers. DIAGRAMS ON PAGE 88

MATERIALS
6 x 8-inch gift box
⅛-inch-wide yellow and gold quilling paper
Card stock: burgundy, light brown, tan, yellow, orange and green
Cardboard
Paper crimper
12-inch paper trimmer
Adhesive foam squares
Double-sided tape
Double-sided adhesive sheets
Clear adhesive dots
Ruler

Wrap package with burgundy card stock. Measure and cut two 1-inch-wide strips from tan paper long enough to wrap around package; add at least 1 inch to length for crimping. Crimp paper strips. Cut two ¾-inch strips of double-sided adhesive; adhere strips onto crimped strips and press onto package about 1 inch from each edge.

Cut two orange card stock strips and three yellow card stock strips ¾ x 11 inches. Fringe long sides of each strip with scissors by cutting halfway through paper. Apply a piece of double-sided tape to one end of paper strip; roll strip to form flower and apply another piece of double-sided tape to close end of roll. Use thumb to pull down fringe to open flower.

Trace and cut out leaf pattern. Fold a piece of green card stock in half and place pattern on folded edge; trace pattern and cut out. Repeat process for four more leaves.

Place a 3¼-inch piece of tape on cardboard and lay eighteen 3-inch lengths of gold quilling paper onto tape; cut ten 3-inch lengths of yellow quilling paper and weave them between the gold quilling strips to form a basket weave.

Draw a rectangle approximately 2 x 3 inches on light brown card stock; cut out and cut slightly angled lines on both sides to form a basket shape. Press paper basket onto a piece of double-sided adhesive sheet; cut out adhesive-covered basket. Remove paper backing; line up bottom of basket to yellow strip on weaving and press onto paper weaving. Remove from cardboard; trim paper edges to fit basket shape.

Cut a 1 x 7-inch piece of light brown card stock and crimp; apply double-sided tape to piece and wrap paper around top section of basket. Adhere piece in back. Adhere foam squares to back of band and attach to package. Referring to photo, adhere flowers and leaves. ■

SOURCES: PeelnStick double-sided adhesive sheets by Therm O Web.

Purple Heart Box

Design by SANDRA GRAHAM SMITH

Sweet Valentine gifts will be cherished when presented in a tiny handmade box. Quick and easy to make, you'll want to treat all your friends!

DIAGRAMS ON PAGE 89

Trace box pattern onto double-sided paper; cut out. Use a ruler and stylus to score dashed lines. Assemble box and glue tab.

Trace one large heart onto light purple patterned paper; cut out and glue to the box heart. Trace one medium heart onto purple patterned paper; cut out and glue to large heart. Trace and cut three small hearts from purple patterned paper; glue to sides and front of box.

MATERIALS
- Double-sided purple patterned paper
- Light purple patterned paper
- Purple patterned paper
- Ruler
- Stylus
- Glue stick

⊢ BOXES ⊣

Flip-Flop Gift Box
Design by LAURIE D'AMBROSIO

MATERIALS
Flip-flop shape papier-mâché box
Pink and black acrylic paints
Small pink flower embellishments
¼-inch-wide pink satin ribbon
Varnish
Liner paintbrush
1-inch wash paintbrush
Adhesive dots
⅛-inch-wide adhesive tape

Fill boxes with tiny treats and hand them out as favors at your next summertime party.

Use the 1-inch wash brush to paint the box, inside and out, black; paint the box lid pink and the box lid edge black. Two or three coats of paint may be needed; let dry between each coat.

Add pink line detail on the box with the liner brush. Once dry, coat both pieces with varnish and let dry completely. Attach flower embellishments to the top with adhesive dots; add a line of ribbon around the edge of the lid with adhesive tape. ■

SOURCES: Flower embellishments from EK Success.

Funky Floral Gift Box

Design by LAURIE D'AMBROSIO

Get the upscale look of beading without the work by adding premade trim to this fun box.

Punch a hole in the center of the lid with the awl. Paint the top of the lid dark pink and the edges blue; paint the bottom of the box and inside dark pink. Paint the bottom sides purple. **Note:** *Use the 1-inch wash brush to paint the box. Use the liner brush for the detail lines.* Two or three coats of paint may be needed; let dry between each coat.

Stamp the flower image onto the center of the lid with purple paint; stamp five more flowers around center and let dry. Place flower template on top of one of the stamped flowers and trace flower with blue colored pencil; go over lines with blue paint. Let dry.

Paint wooden knob blue; let dry. Trace a flower center detail from the template onto top of wooden knob; go over lines with dark pink paint and let dry.

Apply dark pink paint to one petal of the flower stamp; stamp along the entire bottom border of the box. Let dry and add a wavy detail line in border with blue paint.

Once all pieces have completely dried, varnish each and let dry again. Attach the knob to the lid using screwdriver and ¾-inch screw. Attach beaded fringe along the top edge of the lid with double-sided tape. **Note:** *Catch the stitching on the back of the trim with tape so the beads do not fall off.* ∎

SOURCES: Flower stamp and template set from Loew-Cornell; flower fringe trim from Hirschberg Schutz & Co.

MATERIALS
- 8½-inch diameter papier-mâché box
- Acrylic paint: dark pink, blue and purple
- Varnish
- Flower sponge stamp and matching flower template
- Beaded flower fringe trim
- ¼-inch-wide double-sided tape
- Blue colored pencil
- 2-inch diameter unfinished wooden knob
- ¾-inch screw
- 1-inch wash paintbrush
- Liner paintbrush
- Awl
- Screwdriver

Tuscan Book Box

Design by SUSAN STRINGFELLOW

MATERIALS
- Papier-mâché book box
- Green card stock
- Tuscany grape, brown and gold crackle patterned papers
- Burgundy embossed paper
- Gold acrylic paint
- Gold metallic rub-on cream
- Opalescent gold powder
- Gold, burgundy, green and black fibers
- Gold cord
- Gold brads
- Square bronze brad
- Coordinating vintage images
- Gold book corners
- Wine cork
- Small alphabet rubber stamps
- Brown solvent-based ink pad
- Metal decorative embellishment
- Assorted coordinating glass beads
- Small gold bells
- Olive green fabric
- Adhesive foam tape
- Clear dimensional adhesive
- Matte-finish acrylic adhesive medium
- Gloss varnish
- Paintbrushes
- Craft sponge

Pretty enough to be the gift, this embellished papier-mâché book also doubles as a gift box!

Use matte medium to adhere grape patterned paper to front and back of box. To cover the book spine, cut brown patterned paper ¾ inch longer than the length of the spine so paper can be folded over the ends of the book. Dampen the paper slightly before adhering to spine as this will allow paper to be pressed into the ridges. **Note:** *There will be wrinkles in the paper.* Adhere gold crackle patterned paper to the sides of the box, which will be the faux pages of the book.

Paint inside box with gold acrylic paint; let dry. Apply two coats of gloss varnish over paint allowing each coat to dry thoroughly. Lightly dry brush gold paint over the box's faux pages. Add opalescent gold powder to the gloss varnish and paint the entire inside surface of the box; let dry and add one more coat of varnish.

Once box is completely dry, attach gold book corners to box corners. Use craft sponge to apply brown solvent-based ink to two gold brads. Cut eight 16-inch lengths of fibers and gold cord; referring to photo, attach along book spine with sponged gold brads at top and bottom. Allow excess fibers and cord to hang; attach beads and bells to gold cord.

Lightly fold a small piece of olive green fabric and adhere in lower right corner of box. Mat large vintage image onto burgundy embossed paper; rub the edges of embossed paper with gold metallic rub-on cream. Attach decorative metal embellishment in lower left corner of vintage image with clear dimensional adhesive; mount assembled image on top of fabric piece with adhesive foam tape.

Apply brown ink to the edges of a smaller vintage image; mat onto green card stock. Tear the bottom edge and stamp "il vino Italia" onto border; attach to lower left corner of box with square brad. Cut wine cork in half and adhere overlapping small image. ∎

SOURCES: Patterned and embossed papers from Provo Craft; vintage images, book covers and wine cork from Altered Pages; alphabet rubber stamps from Hero Arts; metallic rub-on cream from Craf-T Products; opalescent gold pigment powder from Jacquard Products; Diamond Glaze from JudiKins; Matte Medium from Golden Artist Colors Inc.

Wrapped Santa Gift Box

Design by SANDY ROLLINGER

MATERIALS
- Red, white, black and peach card stock
- Red tissue paper
- Red plaid patterned paper
- Black fine-tip permanent marker
- 4 x 6-inch box
- 1-inch circle punch
- Cellophane tape
- Tracing paper
- Paper trimmer
- Paper crimper
- Small scissors
- Double-sided adhesive sheets
- Adhesive dots

This fun Santa wrap is special enough to become a treasured holiday decor piece! DIAGRAMS ON PAGE 90–91

Place desired gift into box and wrap with red tissue paper. Using provided patterns, trace and cut out shapes on corresponding papers as indicated on patterns. Use paper trimmer to cut enough red plaid patterned paper to fit around box. Attach double-sided adhesive sheets to back of patterned paper; adhere paper around sides of box. Measure a piece of red patterned paper to fit top of box and adhere in same manner.

Adhere top of hat to front of box with a 1-inch square piece of adhesive sheet; repeat for face beneath hat. Cut two 1½-inch strips of white card stock long enough to fit around box; run each through paper crimper. Adhere one crimped strip around box as hat border and remaining strip at bottom of box.

Cut four 1½ x 2-inch strips of white card stock; run each through paper crimper. Cut five 1½ x 2-inch strips of red card stock; crimp. Four of these strips will be Santa's arms and legs. Attach mittens to arms and boots to legs; attach crimped white card stock pieces to arms and legs as trim.

For remaining crimped red card stock piece, cut a 1⅛ x 2½-inch rectangle of white card stock and adhere to crimped piece. Write "to" and "from" on tag; adhere tag to one of Santa's mittens.

Bend ½ inch back on each arm and adhere one to each side of box; adhere legs to bottom of box. Cut a piece of red card stock to fit bottom of box and adhere. Crimp Santa's beard and adhere over face area. Use the 1-inch circle punch to punch a circle from peach card stock and one from white card stock. Crimp the white card stock circle. Use adhesive dots to attach the peach circle to face to form a nose and attach the white circle on top of hat. Draw on eyes with black marker. ■

SOURCES: PeelnStick double-sided adhesive sheets from Therm O Web.

— BOXES —

Star of David Box & Card
Designs by KATHY WEGNER

MATERIALS
- 3 (8½ x 11-inch) sheets navy card stock
- Silver foil paper
- Silver ink pad
- Silver embossing powder
- 3-inch Star of David rubber stamp
- Pillow box die
- Die-cutting machine
- Heat embossing tool
- Double-sided adhesive sheets
- Decorative-edge scissors
- Sandpaper

Stamp on a die-cut box to create a card and bag set with little fuss. Add shimmer with metallic paper and embossing powder.

Use die-cutting machine and pillow box die to cut a box from navy card stock; set aside. Cut a 6-inch square from navy card stock; fold square in half diagonally and set aside. On remaining sheet of card stock, stamp and emboss three Star of David images; let dry.

Place a sheet of silver foil onto sandpaper; press foil with fingertips to add texture to foil. Apply double-sided adhesive sheet to the dull back side of foil and to the three Star of David images.

Cut out Star of David images. Use decorative-edge scissors to cut two 2½ x 4½-inch rectangles and one 4¾ x 4¾ x 6¾-inch triangle from textured foil.

Adhere foil triangle to front of folded square; adhere foil rectangles to both sides of pillow box. Add more texture to foil shapes by pressing sandpaper into foil. **Note:** *Press and lift sandpaper onto foil. Do not rub.* Adhere stars in the center of foil rectangles and on foil triangle. Assemble box using double-sided adhesive. ■

SOURCES: Die and die-cutting machine from AccuCut; PeelnStick double-sided adhesive sheets from Therm O Web.

BOXES

S'mores Surprise

Design by SANDRA GRAHAM SMITH

Tuck tiny presents in this charming stamped snowman bag for some quick cheer in the dreary winter months.

DIAGRAM ON PAGE 92

Enlarge pattern and trace box onto dark green card stock; cut out. Use watermark ink pad to stamp pine branch image randomly over entire surface. Score dashed lines and assemble box; glue top handles together.

Stamp snowman image onto off-white card stock with black ink; color image. Apply white heat-puff paint to marshmallows and heat with embossing tool. Apply gold glitter paint to candle flame; let dry. Cut a small border around image and adhere onto red card stock. Cut around image leaving a small red border. Adhere to center of box. Punch a snowflake out of white craft foam; adhere to handle. ∎

SOURCES: Rubber stamps from Uptown Design Co. and Great Impressions; watermark ink pad from Tsukineko.

MATERIALS
Dark green, red and off-white card stock
Snowman with s'mores rubber stamp
Pine branch rubber stamp
Watermark ink pad
Black ink pad
Snowflake punch
White craft foam
Colored pencils
Gold glitter paint
White heat-puff paint
Heat embossing tool
Glue stick
Ruler
Stylus

Valentine Mini Box

Design by SANDRA GRAHAM SMITH

Sometimes the best things come in small packages, just like this adorable gift box sized for tiny candies or jewelry.

Using the Purple Heart Box patterns on page 89, trace the heart box pattern onto black card stock; cut out. Use a ruler and stylus to score the dashed lines. Fold box to assemble and glue tab.

Trace one large heart onto red card stock; trace three small hearts onto red card stock. Cut out hearts. Center and glue large heart to heart on box; glue small hearts on front and sides of box.

Punch ten hearts from gold metallic paper; glue to box referring to photo for placement. Attach dimensional embellishment to top heart.

SOURCES: Dimensional embellishment from Hot Off The Press.

MATERIALS
Black and red card stock
Gold metallic paper
Small heart punch
Self-adhesive Valentine
    sentiment embellishment
Glue stick
Ruler
Stylus

Valentine Sentiment Box

Design by MARY AYRES

Treat your loved one to a Valentine's Day surprise gift hidden in a romantic box!

Cut tan parchment paper to fit top of lid flap; adhere. Cut rose patterned paper half the size of lid flap; tear left edge and adhere. Punch two 3/16-inch holes through flap. Use craft sponge to apply gold ink to flap edges.

Cut tan parchment paper to fit front of box; cut rose patterned paper half the size of box front. Glue rose patterned paper to parchment paper and apply gold ink to edges. Place paper on box front and mark placement of holes; remove paper and punch holes.

Apply various valentine sentiments to vellum with rub-on transfers; tear rectangles around words leaving space on ends for eyelets. Place rectangles onto mulberry paper and tear mulberry paper edges. Arrange layered rectangles onto parchment/rose paper and attach with gold brads. Glue paper to box.

Cut a 2½ x 4¼-inch rectangle from white card stock; cut top two corners diagonally to form a tag shape. Apply gold ink to edges. Transfer valentine image to mulberry paper; tear paper edges and glue to tag. Apply a valentine sentiment to vellum; tear a 1-inch-wide strip around words. Attach strip diagonally across bottom of tag with brads. Punch a 3/16-inch hole and glue brass bow embellishment at top of tag. Fold box flap over; insert ribbon through holes in box and tag. Tie ribbon into a bow. ■

SOURCES: Gift box and brass embellishment from Plaid/All Night Media; patterned paper from K&Company; rub-on transfers from Royal & Langnickel; Zip Dry paper adhesive from Beacon.

MATERIALS

- 2¾ x 6½ x 9¼-inch gift box
- Rose patterned paper
- Tan parchment paper
- Pink mulberry paper
- White card stock
- White vellum
- 10 small gold brads
- Brass bow embellishment
- ¼-inch-wide dark pink ribbon
- Valentine sentiment rub-on transfers
- Valentine image rub-on transfer
- Gold ink pad
- Craft sponge
- 1/16- and 3/16-inch circle punches
- Instant-dry paper adhesive

Baby Buggy Gift Set

continued from page 6

Baby Buggy Gift Set
S Scroll

Baby Buggy Gift Set
C Scroll

Baby Buggy Gift Set
Teardrop

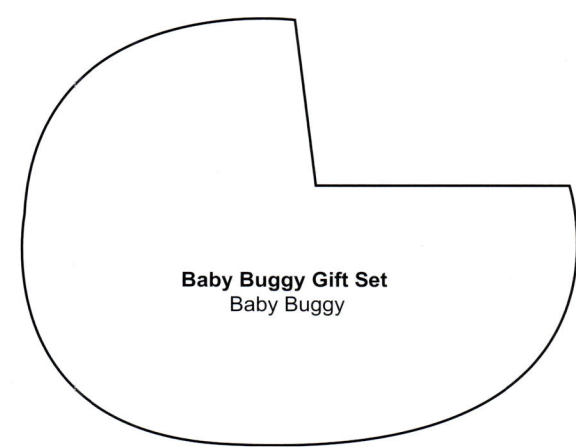

Baby Buggy Gift Set
Baby Buggy

Patriotic Gift Set

continued from page 16

Patriotic Gift Set
Star Pattern

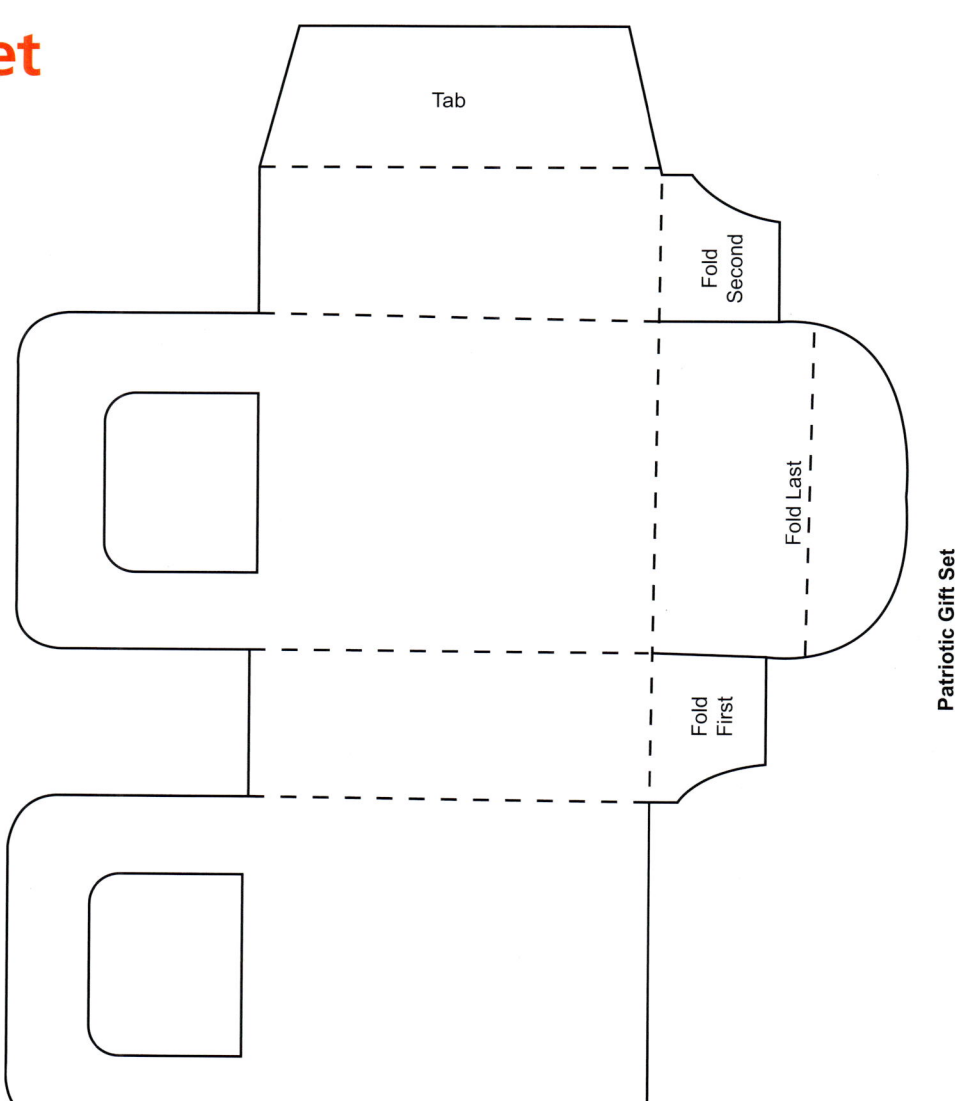

Patriotic Gift Set
Star Box Pattern

Box template courtesy of AccuCut. Reprinted with permission.

Paper Leaves Gift Set

continued from page 18

**Paper Leaves Gift Set
Small Leaf**
Cut 1 from golden
yellow card stock

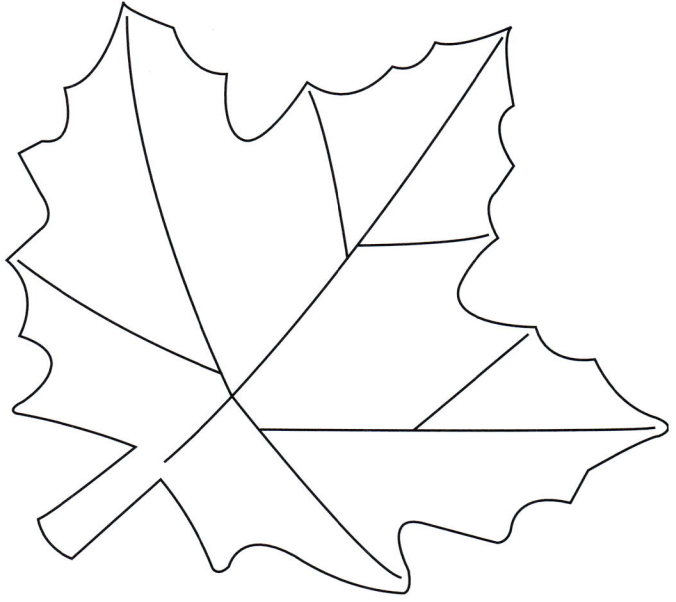

**Paper Leaves Gift Set
Large Leaf**
Cut 1 from golden yellow card stock,
2 from tan card stock and
2 from rust card stock

Teacher Gift Bag

continued from page 19

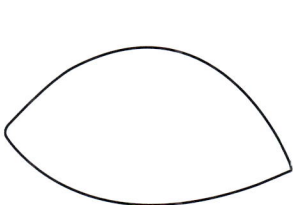

**Teacher Gift Bag
Apple Leaf Pattern**

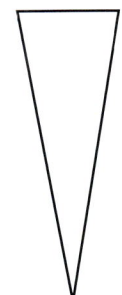

**Teacher Gift Bag
Apple Stem Pattern**

**Teacher Gift Bag
Apple Pattern**

School Days Gift Set

continued from page 20

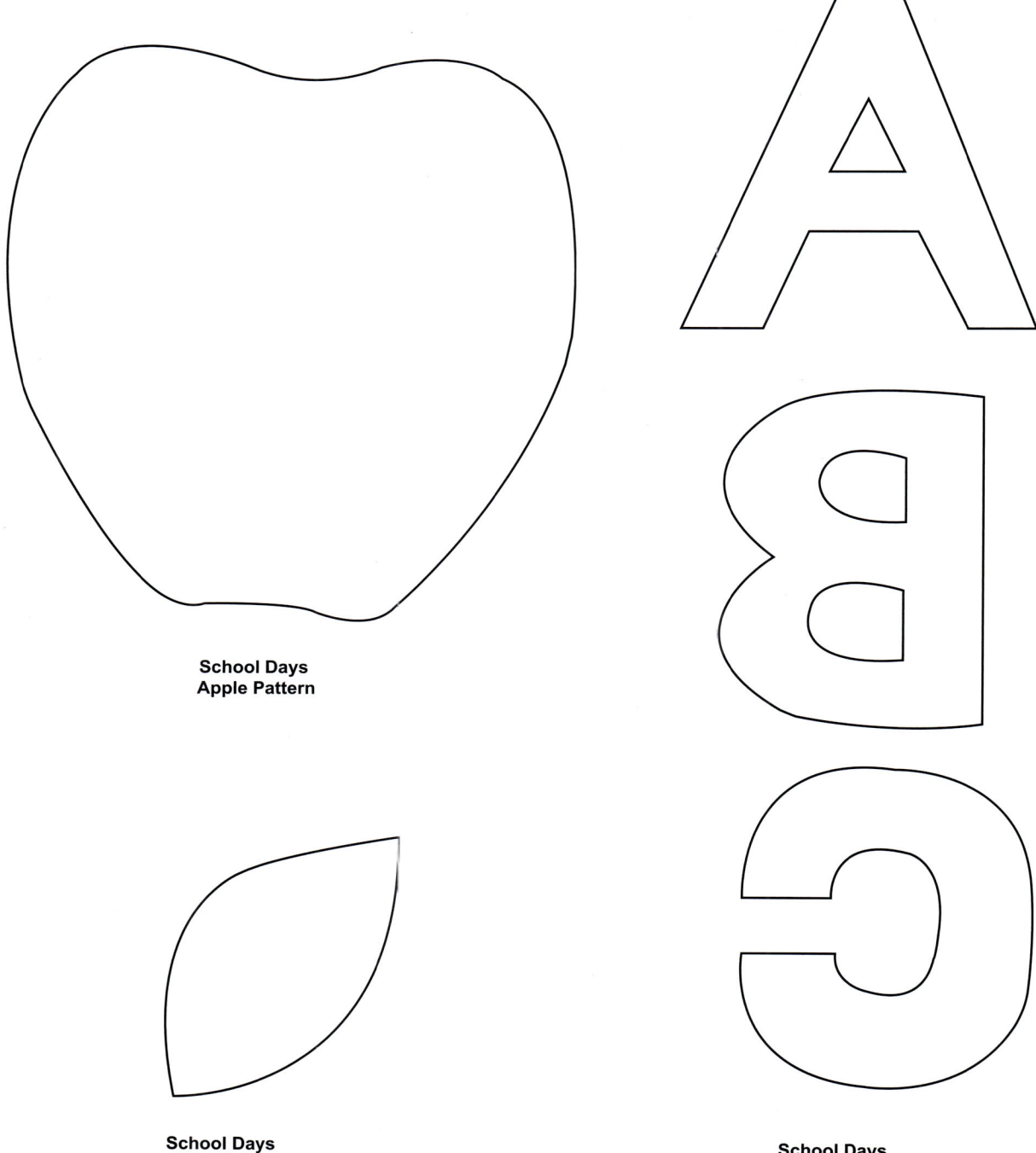

School Days Apple Pattern

School Days Leaf Pattern

School Days Letter Patterns

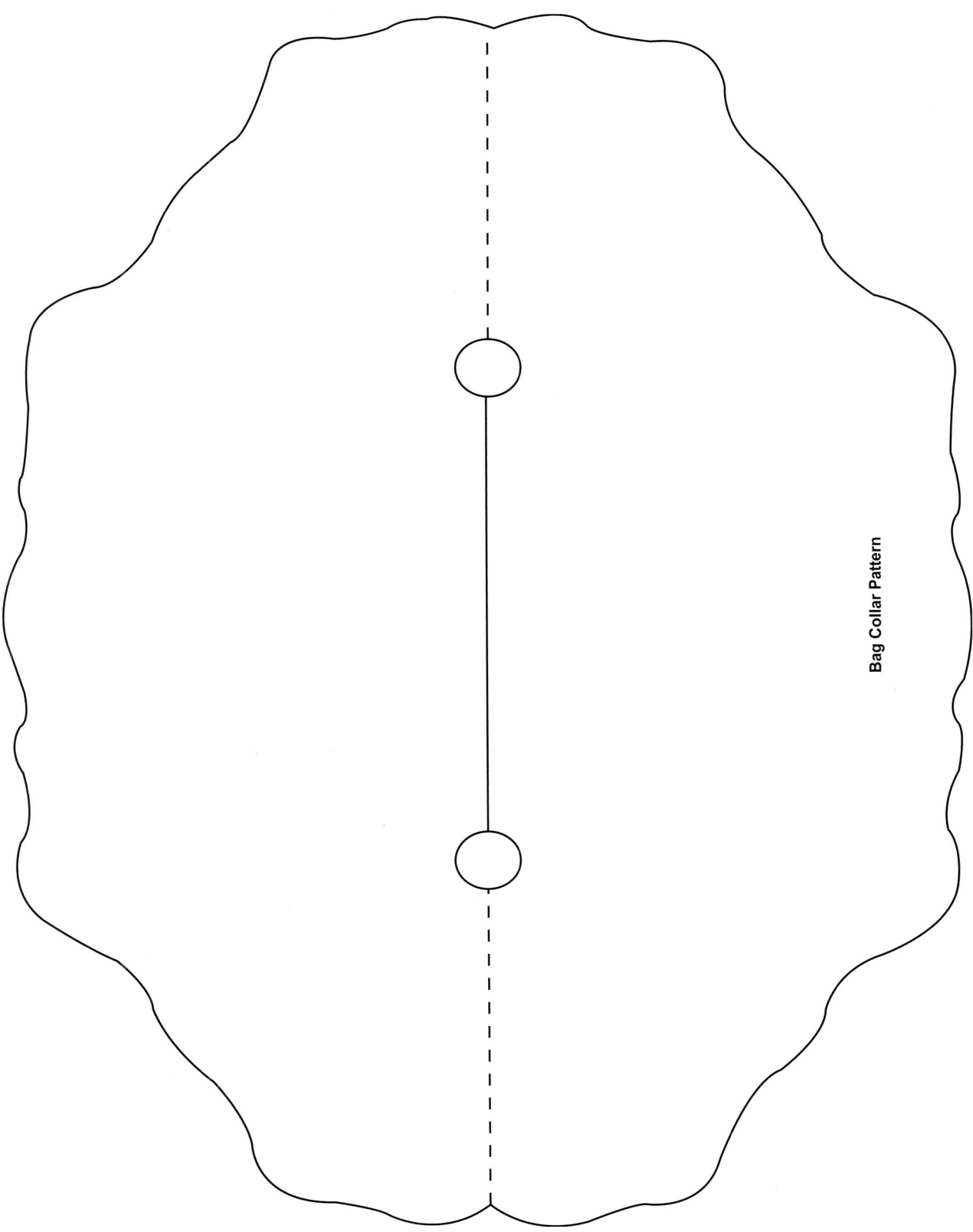

Bag Collar Pattern

DIAGRAMS

Get Ready for Treats!
continued from page 22

Bat
Make 1 for invitation;
make 5 for treat bag

Attach
Bat Here

X

Get Ready for Treats!
Use as shown for invitation;
enlarge designs 152% for
treat bag

⊢ DIAGRAMS ⊢

Gingerbread Gift Bags
continued from page 24

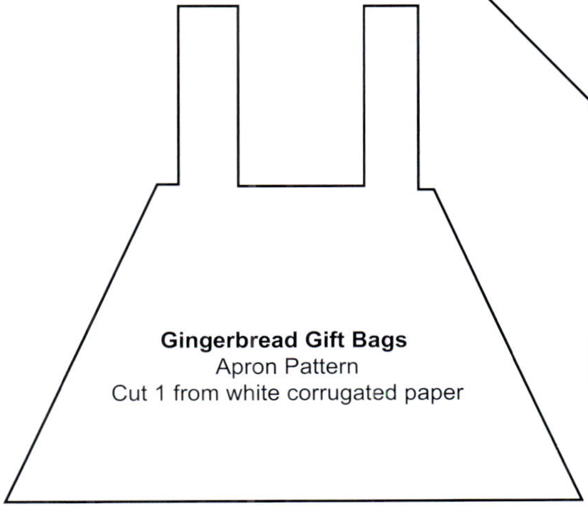

Gingerbread Gift Bags
Heart Pattern
Cut 1 from white poster board
Cut 2 from red or green dotted paper

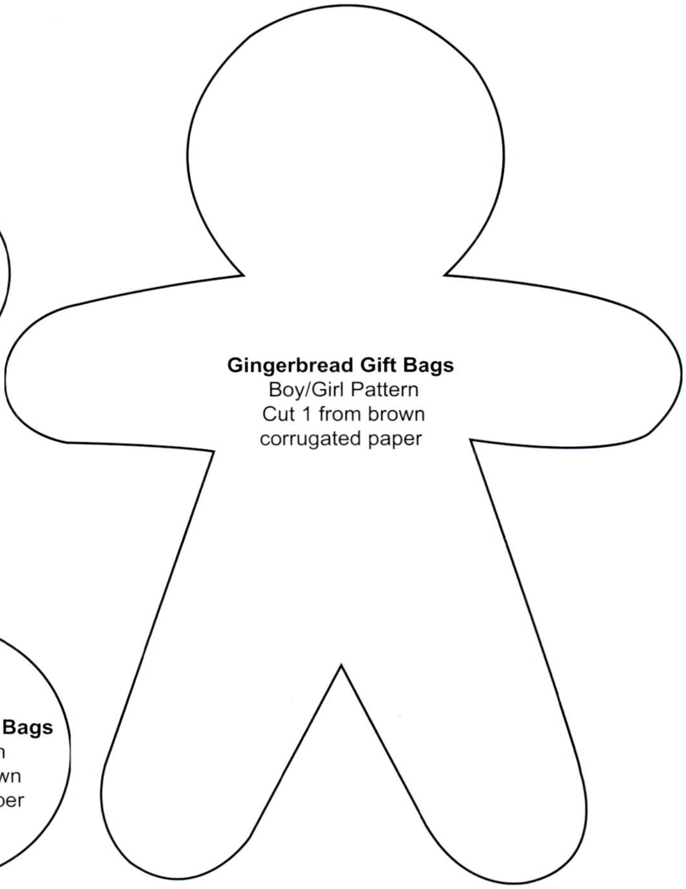

Gingerbread Gift Bags
Boy/Girl Pattern
Cut 1 from brown corrugated paper

Gingerbread Gift Bags
Apron Pattern
Cut 1 from white corrugated paper

Gingerbread Gift Bags
Head Pattern
Cut 1 from brown corrugated paper

Snowman Gift Bag
continued from page 26

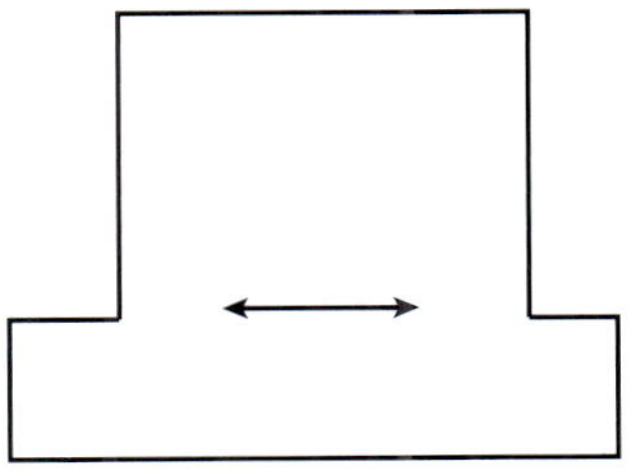

Snowman Gift Bag
Hat Pattern
Cut 1 from black corrugated paper
Arrow denotes direction of corrugated paper

Snowman Gift Bag
Body Pattern
Cut 1 from white corrugated paper
Arrow denotes direction of corrugated paper

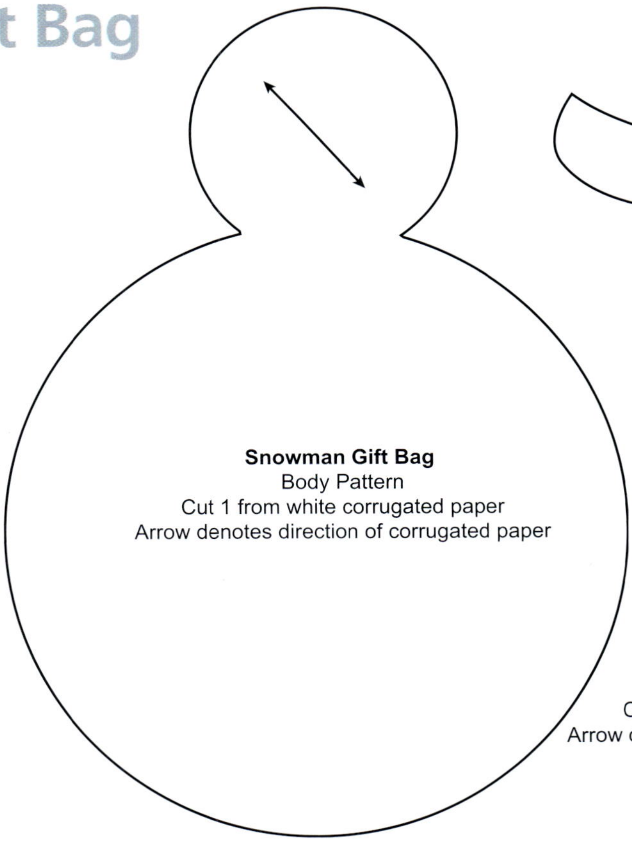

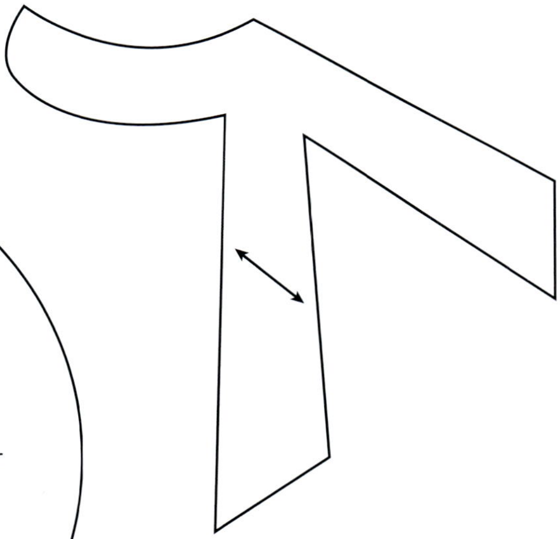

Snowman Gift Bag
Scarf Pattern
Cut 1 from red corrugated paper
Arrow denotes direction of corrugated paper

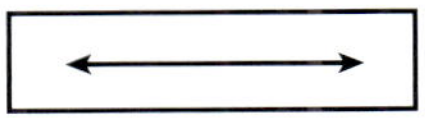

Snowman Gift Bag
Hatband Pattern
Cut 1 from red corrugated paper
Arrow denotes direction of corrugated paper

Annie's Attic, Berne, IN 46711 • AnniesAttic.com • All Wrapped Up

Tiny Treats Bags

continued from page 29

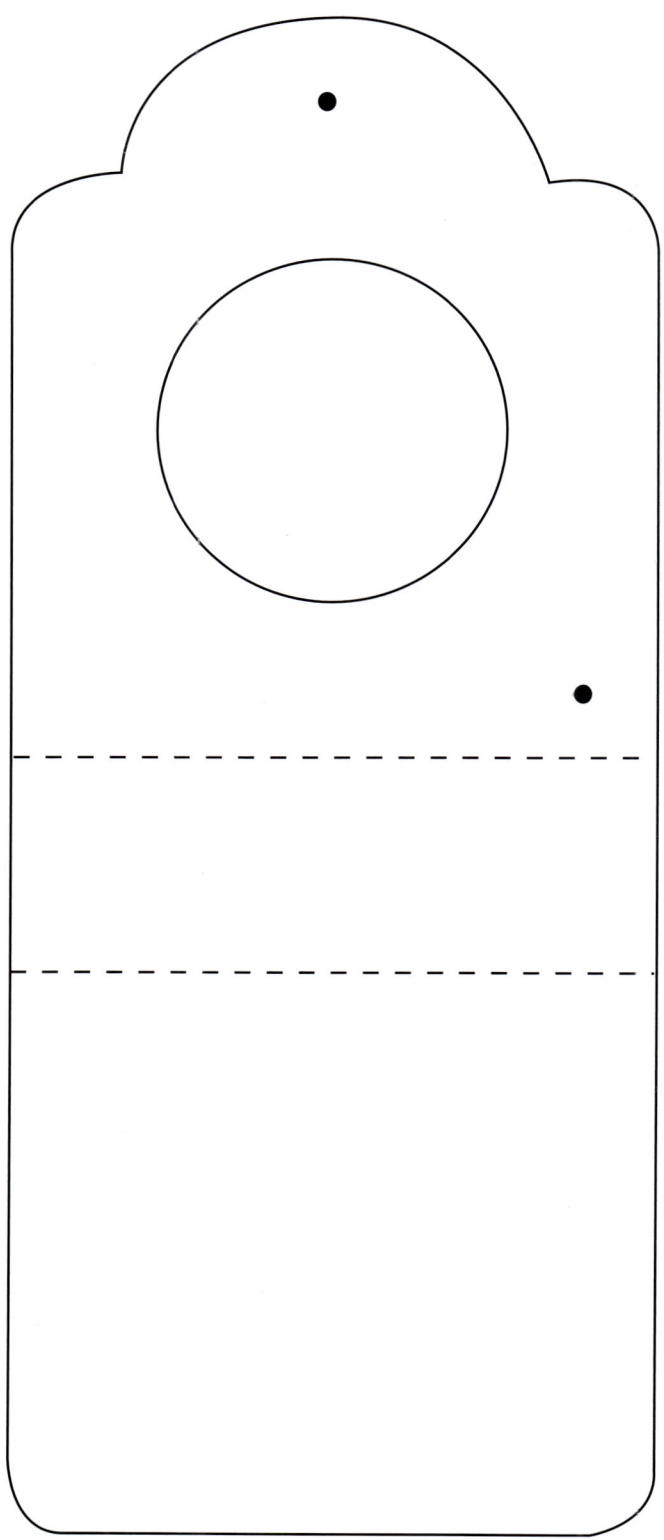

Tiny Treats Bag Pattern

Spirelli Christmas Set
continued from page 30

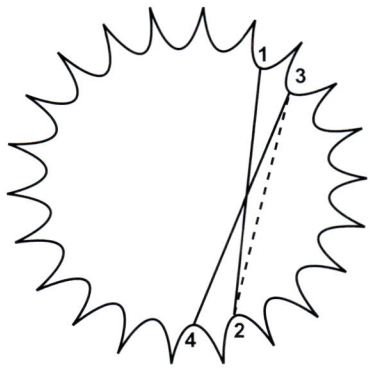

- - - - Thread at back of card
———— Thread at front of card

Spirelli Diagram

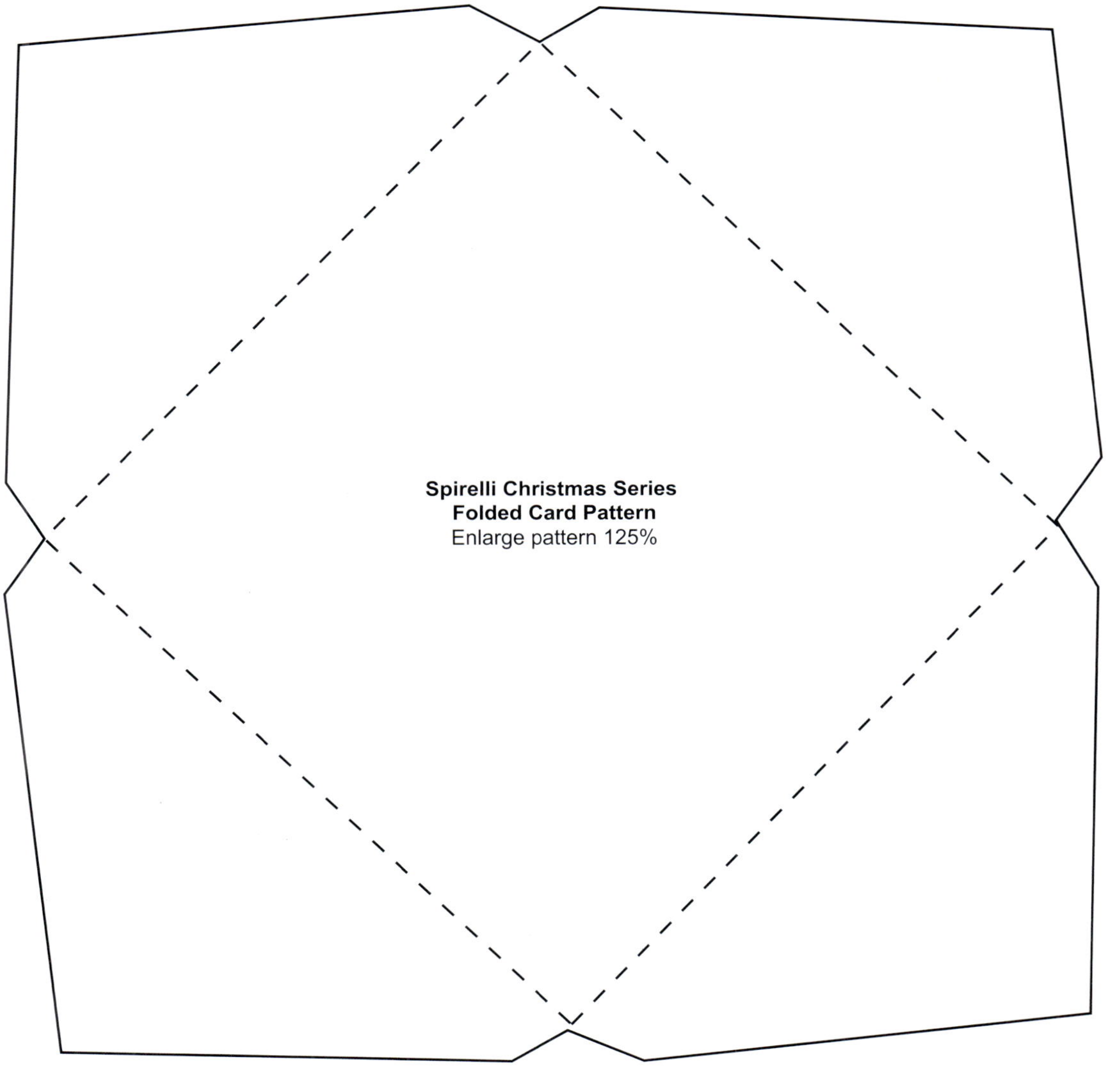

**Spirelli Christmas Series
Folded Card Pattern**
Enlarge pattern 125%

Winter Holidays Paper Purse

continued from page 34

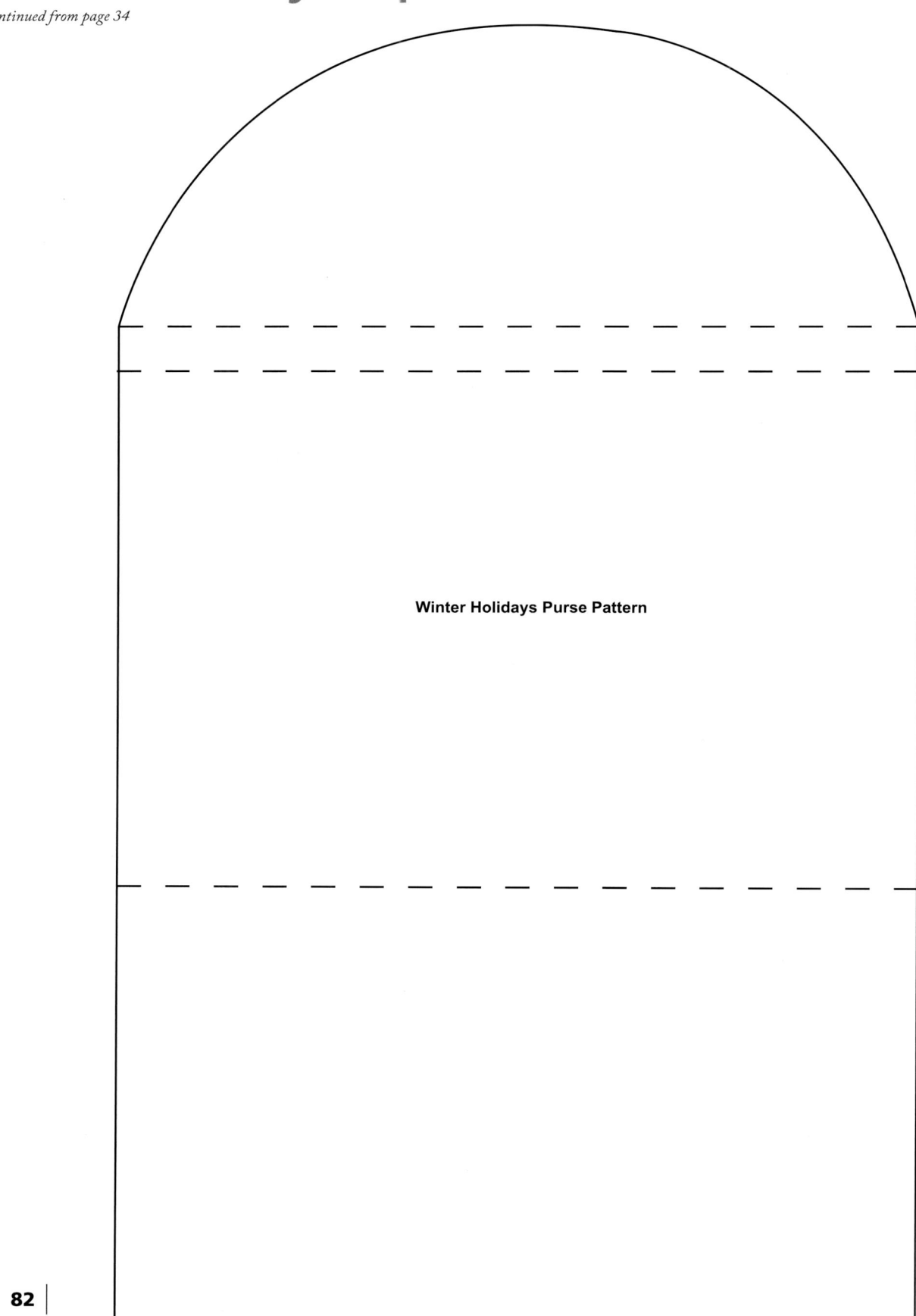

Winter Holidays Purse Pattern

Baby Thank-You Set

continued from page 40

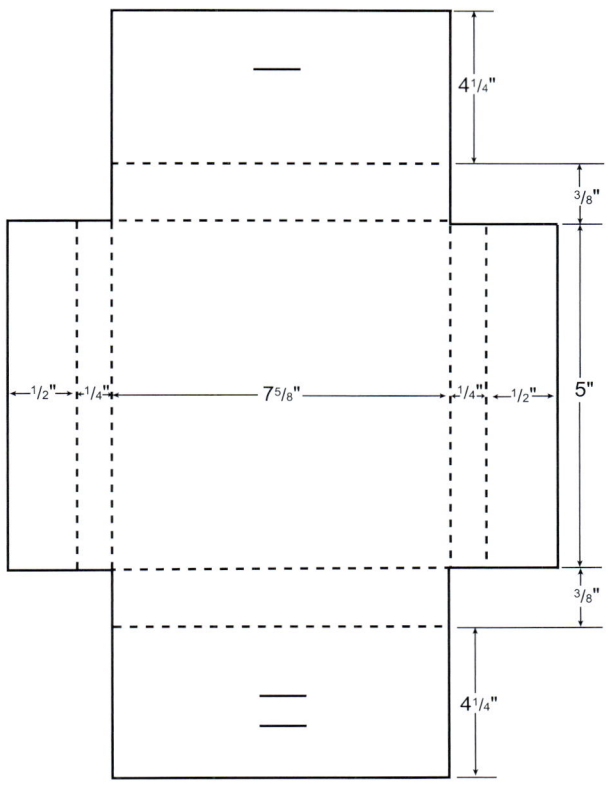

**Baby Thank You
Set Portfolio Diagram**

Dream Stars

continued from page 47

May all
your dreams
come true!

**Dream Stars
Inside Card Verse Pattern**

Birthday Wishes for You!

**Dream Stars
Outside Card Verse Pattern**

**Dream Stars
Star Patterns**

May all your dreams come true!

Nothing Happens Without a Dream
D. Morgan

**Dream Stars
Cloud Patterns**

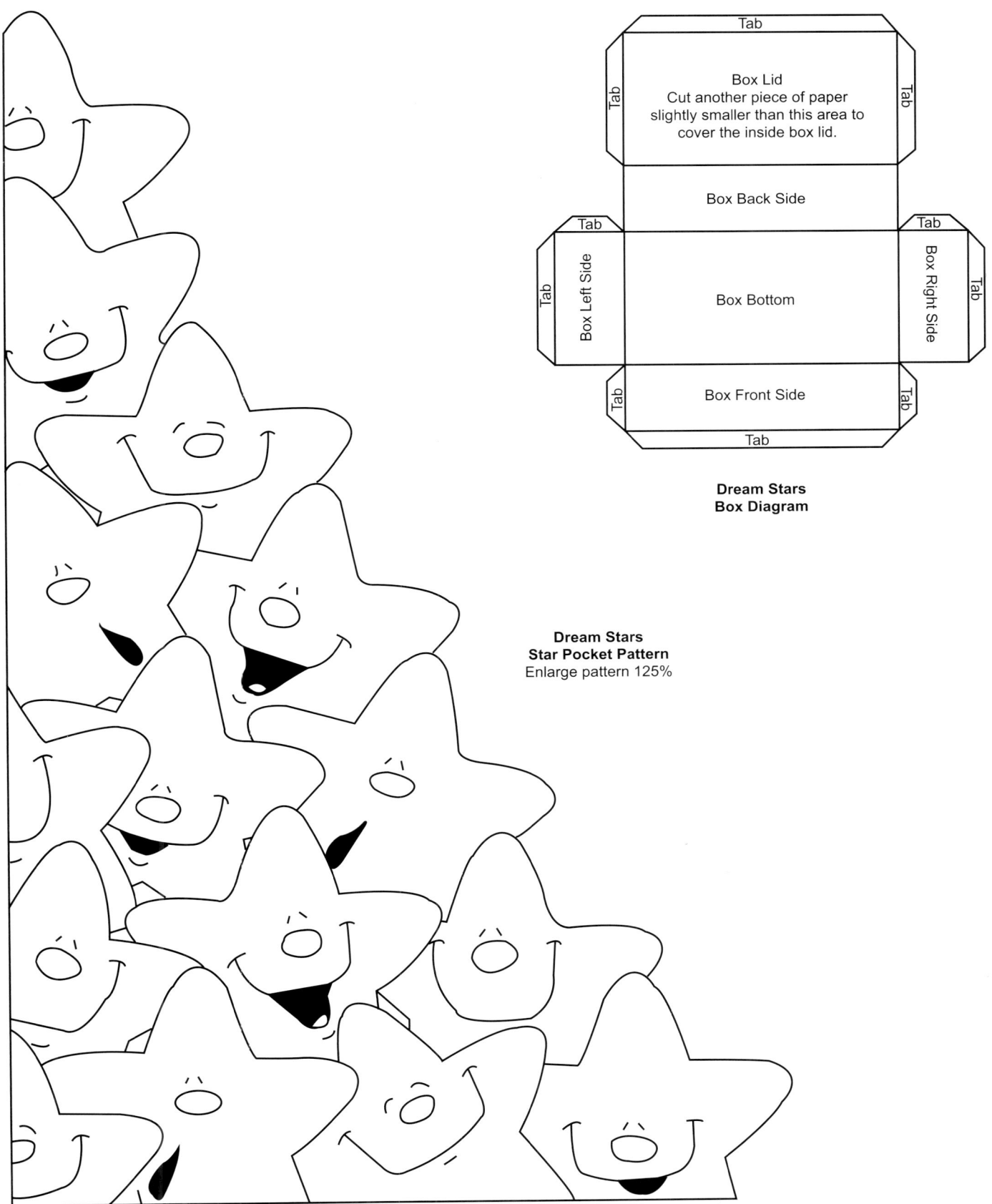

Spooky Paint Cans

continued from page 46

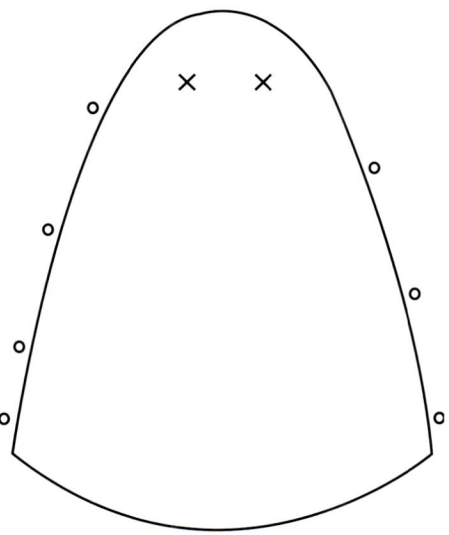

**Spooky Paint Cans
Ghost**

Fruit Gift Set

continued from page 48

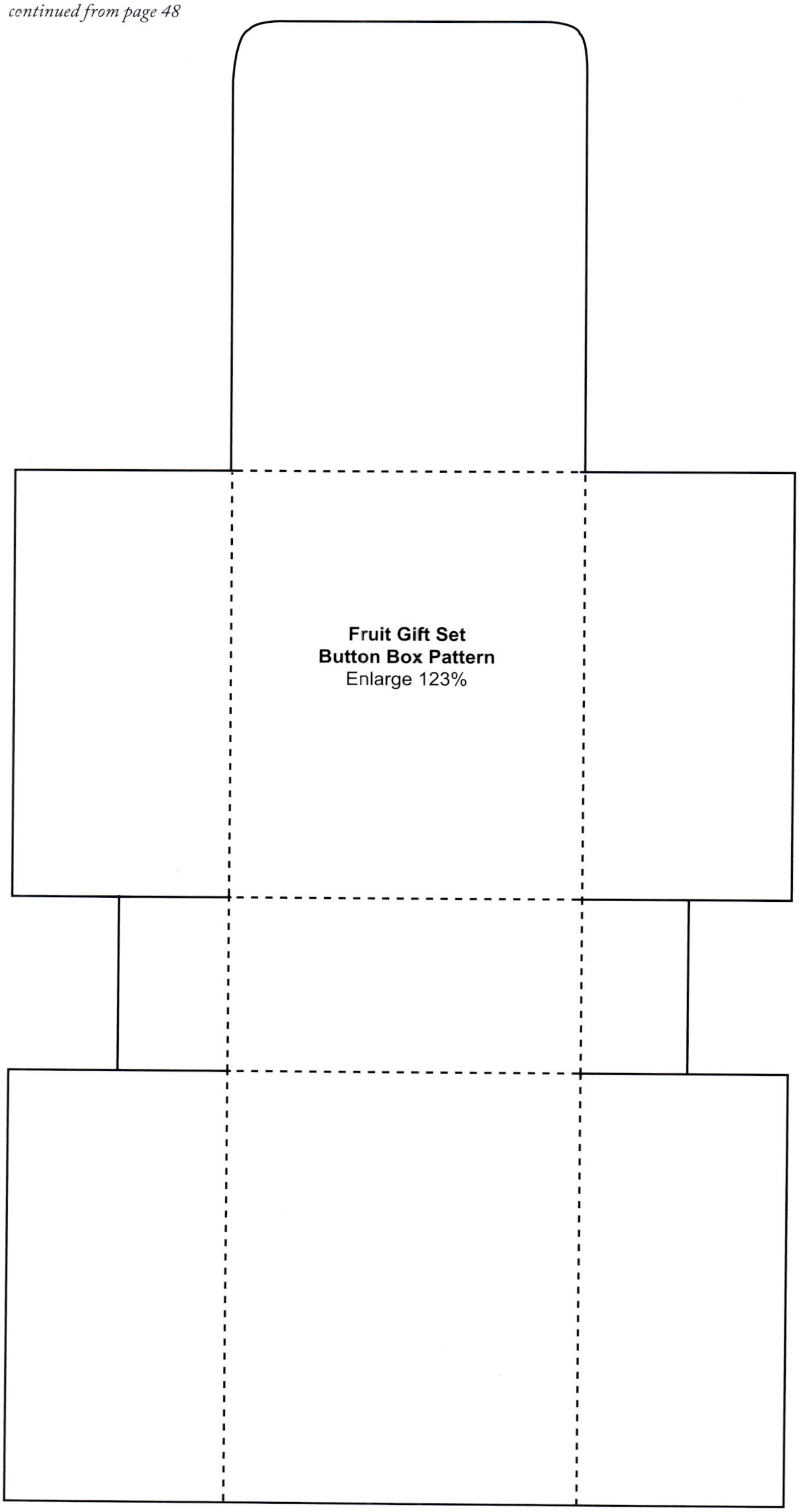

**Fruit Gift Set
Button Box Pattern**
Enlarge 123%

Vellum Heart Totes
continued from page 53

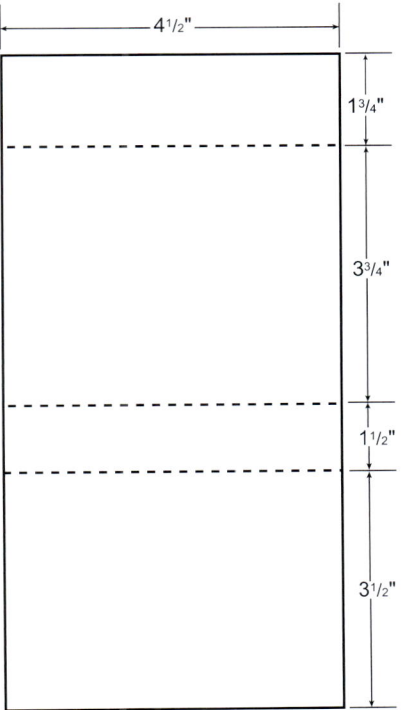

Vellum Heart Totes Diagram

Valentine's Day Party Cones
continued from page 56

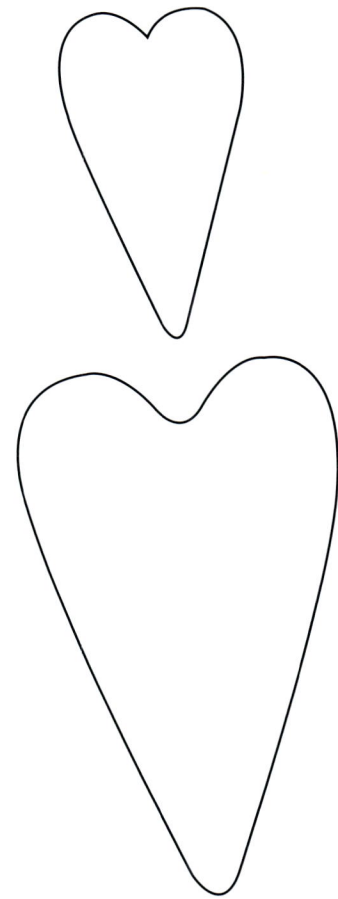

Valentine's Day Party Cones Heart Patterns

Valentine's Day Party Cones Pattern
Enlarge pattern 110%

Folded Floral Gift Set
continued from page 58

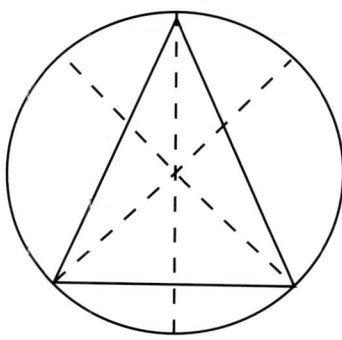

Folded Floral Gift Set Circle Diagram

Paper Marigold Box
continued from page 62

Paper Marigold Box Leaf Pattern

Purple Heart Box

continued from page 63

Purple Heart Box Heart Patterns

Purple Heart Box Pattern

Wrapped Santa Gift Box

continued from page 68

Wrapped Santa Gift Box
Santa Boot
Cut 2 from black card stock

Wrapped Santa Gift Box
Santa Mitten
Cut 2 from red card stock

Wrapped Santa Gift Box
Santa Face
Cut 1 from peach card stock

Wrapped Santa Gift Box
Santa Hat
Cut 1 from red plaid patterned paper

Wrapped Santa Gift Box
Santa Beard
Cut 1 from white card stock

S'mores Surprise
continued from page 71

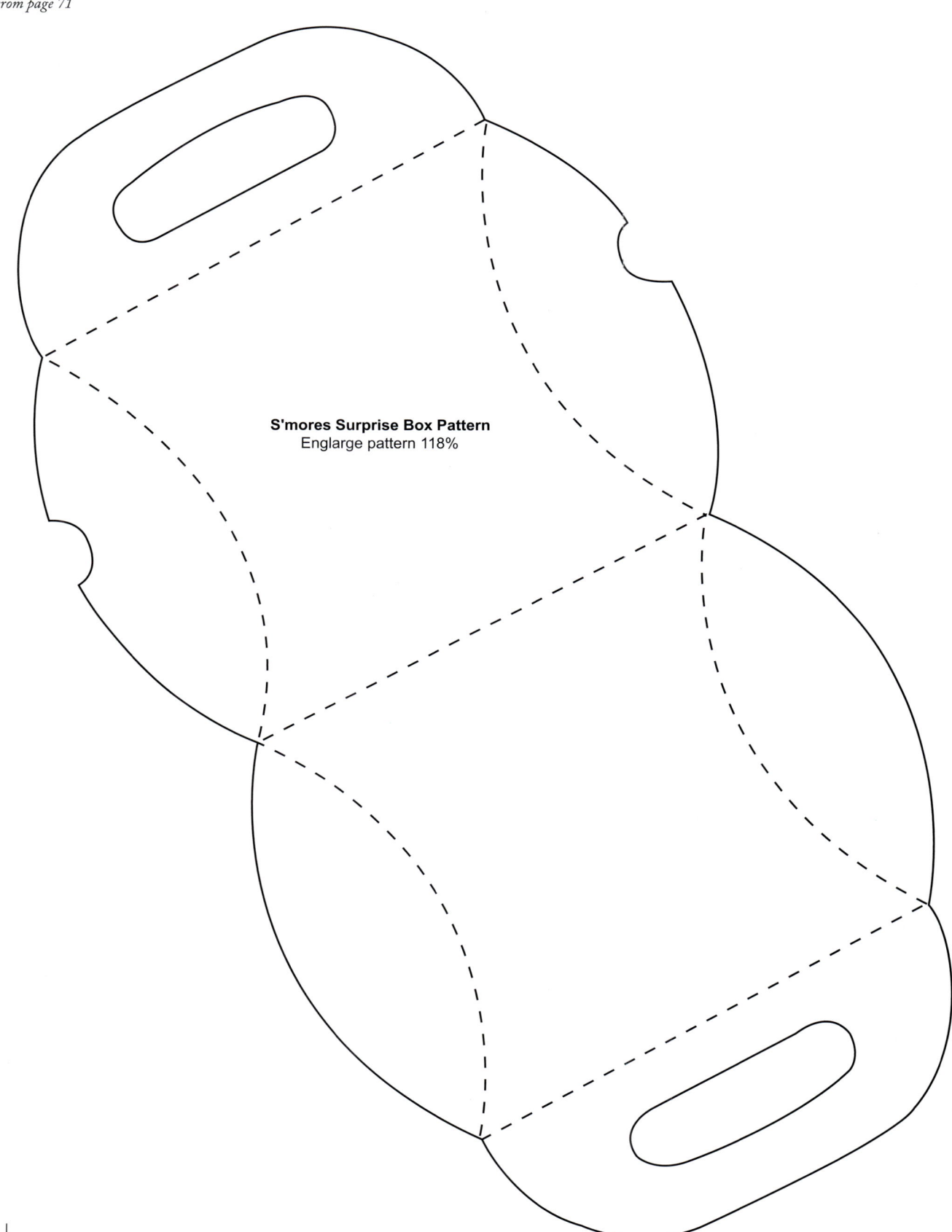

S'mores Surprise Box Pattern
Englarge pattern 118%

⊣ GENERAL INSTRUCTIONS ⊢

Paper Crafting Basics

Paper crafting is easy, creative and fun. Collect basic tools and supplies, learn a few simple terms and techniques, and you're ready to start. The possibilities abound!

Cutting and Tearing

Craft knife, cutting mat Must-have tools. Mat protects work surface, keeps blades from getting dull.
Measure and mark Diagrams show solid lines for cutting, dotted lines for folding.
Other cutters Guillotine and rotary-blade paper cutters, oval and circle cutters, cutters that cut unusual shapes via a gear or cam system, swivel-blade knives that cut along the channels of plastic templates, and die cutting machines (large or small in size and price). Markers that draw as they cut.
Punches Available in hundreds of shapes and sizes ranging from $1/16$ inch to over 3 inches (use for eyelets, lettering, dimensional punch art, and embellishments). Also punches for two-ring, three-ring, coil, comb and disk binding.
Scissors Long and short blades that cut straight or a pattern. Scissors with nonstick coating are ideal for cutting adhesive sheets and tape, bonsai scissors best for cutting rubber or heavy board. Consider comfort—large holes for fingers, soft grips.
Tearing Tear paper for collage, special effects, layering on cards, scrapbook pages and more. Wet a small paintbrush; tear along the wet line for a deckle edge.

Embellishments

If you are not already a pack rat, it is time to start! Embellish projects with stickers, eyelets, brads, nail heads, wire, beads, iron-on ribbon and braid, memorabilia and printed ephemera.

Embossing

Dry embossing Use a light source, stencil, card stock and stylus tool. Add color, or leave raised areas plain.
Heat embossing Use embossing powder, ink, card stock and a heat tool to create raised designs and textures. Powders come in a wide range of colors. Fine grain is called "detail" and heavier called "ultrathick." Embossing powders will not stick to most dye inks—use pigment inks or special clear embossing inks for best results.

Glues and Adhesives

Basics Each glue or adhesive is formulated for a particular use and specified surfaces. Read the label and carefully follow directions, especially those that involve personal safety and health.
Foam tape adds dimension.
Glue dots, adhesive sheets and cartridge type machines quick grab, no drying time needed.
Glue pens Fine line control.
Glue sticks Wide coverage.
Repositionable products Useful for stencils and temporary holding.

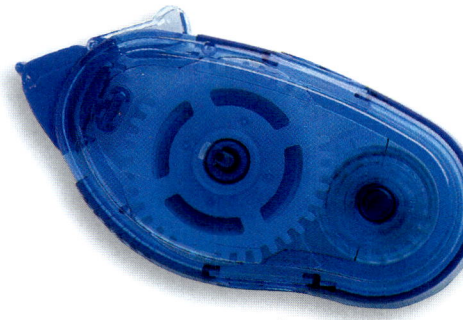

GENERAL INSTRUCTIONS

Measuring

Rulers A metal straightedge for cutting with a craft knife (a must-have tool). Match the length of the ruler to the project (shorter rulers are easier to use when working on smaller projects).

Quilter's grid ruler Use to measure squares and rectangles.

Pens and Markers

Choose inks (permanent, watercolor, metallic, etc.), **colors** (sold by sets or individually), **and nibs** (fine point, calligraphy, etc.) **to suit the project.** For journals and scrapbooks, make sure inks are permanent and fade-resistant.

Store pens and markers flat unless the manufacturer says otherwise.

Scoring and Folding

Folding Mountain folds—up, valley folds—down. Most patterns will have different types of dotted lines to denote mountain or valley folds.

Tools Scoring tool and bone folder. Fingernails will scar the surface of the paper.

Paper and Card Stock

Card stock Heavier and stiffer than paper. A sturdy surface for cards, boxes, ornaments.

Paper Lighter weight surfaces used for drawing, stamping, collage.

Storage and organization Store paper flat and away from moisture. Arrange by color, size or type. Keep your scraps for collage projects.

Types Handmade, milled, marbled, mulberry, origami, embossed, glossy, matte, botanical inclusions, vellum, parchment, preprinted, tissue and more.

Stamping

Direct-to-paper (DTP) Use ink pad, sponge or stylus tool to apply ink instead of a rubber stamp.

Inks Available in pads and re-inker bottles. Types include dye and pigment, permanent, waterproof and fade resistant or archival, chalk finish, fast drying, slow drying, rainbow and more. Read the labels to determine what is best for a project or surface.

Make stamps Carve rubber, erasers, carving blocks, vegetables. Heat Magic Stamp foam blocks to press against textures. Stamp found objects such as leaves and flowers, keys and coins, etc.

Stamps Sold mounted on wood, acrylic or foam, or unmounted (rubber part only), made from vulcanized rubber, acrylic or foam.

Store Flat and away from light and heat.

Techniques Tap the ink onto the stamp (using the pad as the applicator) or tap the stamp onto the ink pad. Stamp with even hand pressure (no rocking) for best results. For very large stamps, apply ink with a brayer. Color the surface of a stamp with watercolor markers (several colors), huff with breath to keep the colors moist, then stamp; or lightly spray with water mist before stamping for a very different effect.

Unmounted stamps Mount temporarily on acrylic blocks with Scotch Poster Tape on one surface (nothing on the rubber stamp) or one of the other methods (hook and loop, paint on adhesives, cling plastic).

Buyers Guide

Buyers Guide Check with your local retail store for availability. If you can't find a product contact the manufacturer directly to find a shop in your area.

AccuCut, Customer Care Center, 1035 E. Dodge St., Fremont, NE 68025, (800) 288-1670

Altered Pages, www.alteredpages.com

American Traditional Designs, 442 First New Hampshire Turnpike, Northwood, NH 03261, (800) 278-3624

Anna Griffin Inc., 733 Lambert Drive, Atlanta, GA 30324, www.annagriffin.com

BagWorks Inc., 3301-C S Cravens Road, Fort Worth, TX 76119

Beacon Adhesives Inc., 125 MacQuestan Parkway S., Mount Vernon, NY 10550, (914) 699-3400

Biblical Impressions, (877) 587-0941, www.biblical.com

Blumenthal Lansing Co., 1929 Main St., Lansing, IA 52151

The C-Thru Ruler Co./Deja Views, 6 Britton Drive, Box 356, Bloomfield, CT 06002

Colors by Design, (800) 832-8436, www.colorsbydesign.com

Craf-T Products, www.craf-tproducts.com

Creative Beginnings, www.creativebeginnings.com

Creative Crystals Co., 6222 Tower Lane, Suite B-7, Sarasota, FL 34240

DecoArt, P.O. Box 386, Stanford, KY 40484, (800) 367-3047

Delta Technical Coatings/Rubber Stampede, 2550 Pellissier Place, Whittier, CA 90601

Denami Design, www.denamidesign.com

DieCuts With a View, 2250 North University Parkway, Provo, UT 84604, (801) 224-6766

DMD, Inc., 2300 S. Old Missouri Road Springdale, AR 72764, (800) 805-9890

Doodlebug Design Inc., (801) 966-9952, www.doodlebugdesigninc.com

Duncan Enterprises, 5673 E. Shields Ave., Fresno, CA 93727, (800) 438-6226

Duro Art Industries Inc., 1832 Juneway Terrace, Chicago, IL 60626

Ecstasy Crafts, www.ecstasycrafts.com

EK Success Ltd., 125 Entin Rd., Clifton, NJ 07014

Emagination Crafts, 463 W. Wrightwood Ave., Elmhurst, IL 60126

Fiskars, 7811 W. Stewart Ave., Wausau, WI 54401-8027

Great Impressions Rubber Stamps, 220 W. Center St., Centralia, WA 98531

Golden Artist Colors Inc., 188 Bell Road, New Berlin, NY 13411-9527, (800) 959-6543

Hero Arts Rubber Stamps, 1343 Powell St., Emeryville, CA 94608

Hirschberg Schutz & Co. Inc., (908) 810-1111

Hot Off The Press Inc., 1250 N.W. Third, Canby, OR 97013

Jacquard Products: Rupert, Gibbon & Spider, Inc., P.O. Box 425, Healdsburg, CA 95448, (800) 442-0455

JudiKins, www.judikins.com

K&Company, 8500 N.W. River Park Drive, Pillar #136, Parkville, MO 64152

KI Memories, www.kimemories.com

Kreinik Mfg. Co. Inc., 3106 Lord Baltimore Drive, Suite 101, Baltimore, MD 21244, www.kreinik.com

Krylon/Sherwin-Williams Co., Craft Customer Service, W. 101 Prospect Ave., Cleveland, OH 44115

Loew-Cornell, 563 Chesnut Ave., Teaneck, NJ 07666-2490

LuminArte, 3322 W. Sussex Way, Fresno, CA 93727, (866) 229-1544

Magenta Rubber Stamps, www.magentarubberstamps.com

Magic Mesh, P.O. Box 8, Lake City, MN 55041, (651) 345-6374

Making Memories, 1168 W. 500 N., Centerville, UT 84014, (801) 294-0430

Me & My Big Ideas, 20321 Valencia Circle Lake Forest, CA 92630

New Dimensions, www.newdimensionspaper.com

Nicole Crafts, www.nicolecrafts.com

NRN Designs, www.nrndesigns.com

Offray, (800) 551-LION

Plaid/All Night Media, 3225 Westech Drive, Norcross, GA 30092

Provo Craft/Sizzix, mail-order source: **Creative Express,** 295 W. Center St., Provo, UT 84601-4436

Renaissance Art Stamps, P.O. Box 1218, Burlington, CT 06013

Royal & Langnickel, www.royalbrush.com

Stampabilities, www.stampabilities.com

Stampin' Up!, (800)-STAMPUP, www.stampinup.com

Therm O Web, 770 Glenn Ave., Wheeling, IL 60090, (847) 520-5200

Toner Plastics, 699 Silver St., Agawam, MA 01001

Tsukineko Inc., 17640 N.E. 65th St., Redmond, WA 98052, (800) 769-6633, www.tsukineko.com

Uptown Design Co., 1000 Town Center, Suite 1 Browns Point, WA 98422

The Buyer's Guide listings are provided as a service to our readers and should not be considered an endorsement from this publication.

Designer Listing & Project Index

American Traditional Stencils
Snowman Set, 27
Santa Set, 28

Mary Ayres
Spooky Paint Cans, 46
Winter Gift Pail, 54
Glass Petal Tins, 57
Valentine Sentiment Box, 73

Laurie D'Ambrosio
Beaded Gift Bag, 15
Stamped Bubble Mailer, 33
Elegant Snowflake Bag, 36
Itty Bitty Surprise Card, 51
Flip-Flop Gift Box, 64
Funky Floral Gift Box, 65

DMD
Graduation Memories, 44

Margaret Hanson-Maddox
Vellum Heart Totes, 53

Jacqueline Jones
Baby Thank-You Set, 40
Fruit Gift Set, 48

Annie Lang
Get Ready for Treats!, 22
Chick Flick DVD Wrap, 41
Dream Stars, 42
Halloween Fun CD Pocket, 50
Winter Memories, 52

Mary Lynn Maloney
Wrapped Soaps, 38
Colorful Candle Band, 39

Lorine Mason
Folded Floral Gift Set, 58

Loretta Mateik
Love Gift Bag, 37
Valentine's Day Party Cones, 56

Marilynne Oskamp
Spirelli Christmas Series, 30

Kathleen Paneitz
Party-Time Set, 12

Helen Rafson
Teacher Gift Bag, 19
Gingerbread Gift Bags, 24
Snowman Gift Bag, 26

Sandy Rollinger
Wedding Gift Trio, 4
Baby Buggy Gift Set, 6
Masculine Gift Bag, 9
Winter Holidays Paper Purse, 34
Baby Carriage Gift Box, 60
Paper Marigold Box, 62
Wrapped Santa Gift Box, 68

Sandra Graham Smith
The Great Outdoors Set, 10
Glamour Girl Set, 14
Patriotic Gift Set, 16
School Days Gift Set, 20
Tiny Treats Bags, 29
Purple Heart Box, 63
S'mores Surprise, 71
Valentine Mini Box, 72

Susan Stringfellow
Spring Butterfly Bag, 3
Fish Gift Bag, 8
"Pour Vous" Gift Bag, 17
Tuscan Book Box, 67

Kathy Wegner
Paper Leaves Gift Set, 18
Star of David Box & Card, 70